RescueSam

IS THIS EVEN DATING ANYMORE?

Samantha Holland

PAGE PUBLISHING, INC.
Conneaut Lake, PA

First originally published by Page Publishing 2020

ISBN 978-1-64628-133-6 (pbk)
ISBN 978-1-64628-134-3 (digital)

Printed in the United States of America

INTRODUCTION

I have been married and divorced twice now. The first time in my twenties, and the second unexpectedly in my thirties. I never really enjoyed being single, but I can promise it gets harder the older you get. Times are changing, and there has been a monumental paradigm shift in the format of dating. I was thrown back into it and have been trying to navigate my way through just like everyone else. It has been about as easy as flying a kite in a tornado. I started writing because no one could believe my stories were real! Then I thought about all the other people out there thinking that they were the only ones going through this. You are not alone. Dating is hard for just about everyone, so sit back, pour a cocktail, and enjoy my journey of discovery. I can only hope that out of all my trials, you learn something or at the very least be entertained!

CHAPTER ONE

Swipe Right for Profile: An Introduction into Online Dating

From the Mouth of Baes

I wanted to start first with the one subject that haunts me and delights me all the time: communication! Let's be honest, men excel in so many areas, but 99.9 percent of the time, communication is not one of them. Men make fun of women constantly for sitting around and talking about feelings, but we get the info out. I, myself, always choose the direct route, but it seems with men this is where I go wrong. But more about that later.

I'm choosing to start with what men have been saying to me. Most of my dating experiences have been with online dating. It all starts with an initial message, and that is where so many go so wrong. Occasionally I see men in public, and they have interesting things to say as well. For example, I saw a man I know, conversation is happening—casual—then he proceeds to tell me about a new, over-the-counter sexual enhancement drug that makes a man "hard for at least five hours," then proceeds to tell me: "I don't need that shit. I'm so horny all the time. I wanna f——everything I see," as he's looking me in my face (eye contact is important in communication). Charming as always "Mr. Strong like bull."

Then we have my very first date after becoming single; it was bound to be a winner. The guy tells me, "I've never dated a woman who weighs more than me, and her ass has to fit the pinky rule." He then touches his thumbs together and extends his pinky's out. "If her ass can't fit within my pinkies, she's too big to ride my bike, and I won't date her." (I was listening and reaching for another slice of pizza—interesting). We stayed in contact for a while after but never went out again.

Don't get me wrong, some are charming about as genuine as an overseas IRS debt notifications company cold-calling to inform that you owe the IRS thousands and the police are on the way. The compliments always flow, saying that I'm pretty, beautiful, a queen, on and on. I've had marriage proposals since they knew from my five pics and bio that I was the one. The offers for sex, as one of them wrote S-E-X, are never ending. Men are always asking if I'm "horny" or if I'd like to "watch them in the shower" and so much more.

One of the best has been the guy who started off talking about dogs and how his dog has a bad habit of humping visitors, especially women. Then proceeded to ask if on our date, I would (I'm paraphrasing) "allow his dog to hump me until he finished while he watched." Let that soak in, and if it does, hydrogen peroxide and dawn are excellent stain removers. LOL *I have been called all the following* (and then some): bitch, whore, slut, cunt, prude, snob, tease, n——, that I will forever be alone, that I'm too picky, that I think I'm better than everyone else, and that I'm not shit. Been yelled at from my parking lot: "I've driven out here twice, and you didn't even put out," "Everyone double parties you just have your own war on drugs." Those last few were from a guy I went out with twice. We'll call him Mr. Mix and Snooze. I could write a whole chapter about that disaster date! I've been told that I'm amazing, and they can't understand why I'm single.

All this and more has been my experience over the past few years, and I'm here to share now. Because if all these guys have one thing in common, it's the fact that I'm quick to screenshot, and I can write!

Second Opinions

Dating profiles are now the new "first impression." You flip through pics, one maybe more, hopefully read the attached bio (if there is one), and make a split-second decision. So the importance of your first impression is paramount. *You* will be judged for what you put out there and how it looks. You know that the old saying is true, "A picture is worth a million words" or, in a few cases, "A million warning flags."

So it would be safe to say that getting your profile proofread and a second opinion would be a great idea. I know that I have done it for several people including guys at work and even one of those occasions got me divorced. Long story but true! So to stay true to my title for this one, I'm going to share with you just a glimpse into some of the "pickup lines," "one-liners," "conversation starters," profile names, and profile catch lines that I have come across.

Now I do feel like I must preface with the fact there have been some really cool, funny, and interesting messages. Some of those even lead to dates. I also understand that taking a chance and initiating conversation can be scary and takes an amount of bravery, so to all the guys who write me every day, thank you, because if nothing else, you provide me with more material. PS Grammar should always count!

"Good morning, snow bunny. How you doing today? Let's be cool and hangout. Do you like chocolate men and sports? Let's go dancing and drinking together. Do you like hip-hop and R & B? Let's work out together? Let's talk." Now this one isn't so bad. I mean other than some grammatical errors, referring to African Americans as chocolate, and being all over the place, he was respectful.

"Hi, sexy, I like you so much. I wanna make you happy tonight LOL." Okay, so a bit creepy, especially since I'm pretty sure he didn't mean emotionally happy.

Profile tag line reads: "You love the wrong man. That's what wrong with you." Why thank you, kind sir. I was wondering what was wrong with me. Next tag line: "Feel my all black aura wen i step up in dis s———." Now I give him points for "aura." I don't really pretend to understand the rest, and I don't really know what he's stepping up in?

This next gentleman lists his profession as "Chief Executive Officer." I really hope it's not for a company's HR department since his tag line reads: "Majority of you Women Now Days Lie 2 much." Is it just me but bashing the opposite sex doesn't usually draw them in? Another is: "Looking for a playmate. Open for anything." Unless you're talking about the park and kids, let's not start anything with "playmate," but hey, at least he's putting his intentions out there. Some are a little more flattering: "You are really pretty! Are you real?" Now as a knee-jerk reaction, he got a sarcastic answer back, but it was an attempt at a compliment. This next is a combination of tag line and message. Tag line: "———I tell you, and you ain't gone love." Can I get an interpreter for this one? His message to me is: "You can write yours in the sand on the sky I'mma write mines in the dirt." Yup, that's verbatim what he wrote.

My tag line for those wondering what witty number I came up with is a line from a country song that says, "Are we writing our names in the sand or in the stars." So to be fair, a lot of guys use that as an opener.

So here is an example of a response and the three messages he sent me without me responding, "Yes and making a sandcastle LOL. Hey, you can't handle me anyways." *Ooohhhh*, you got me there, dude! You're probably right; I couldn't handle your mad sandcastle-building skills almost as important as nun chuck skills.

Tag lines continued: "Sugar mommy? I'm twenty-five, babes." I feel like it's too soon in our relationship to start using pet names (WTF). Next, this stud's tag line was, "Looking for me!" Under profession was, "Making your panties wet." Well, at least he has goals. His interest included: women, porn, sex, money, music, and life; and this is his *ooohhh*-so charming bio: "I'm not on here for games or bullshit. I keep being messed with by everyone, and they think it's cool for me to suffer as if I don't really know I have haters that play to many games and mind f——me. Let's seriously live life on the edge and let's hook up ASAP." Now if this man isn't issue-free, I don't know who is.

I will leave off with this last charmer who pretty much had a whole conversation with himself, seven messages to my one response. Ready?

"69"

My response "23x3?" (Maybe he wanted to play a math game?) The rest are his: "Wya," "please," "where r u," "I wanna eat your pussy," "Wya sexy."

Damn that compliment at the end almost hooked me. LOL better luck next time fisherman. And damn if my spell-check didn't have a hard time trying to figure out what was really happening here. LOL.

Chemistry Tutor Needed, 5'10" and Above

Chemistry is a funny thing in relationships. It's needed for any relationship to start to build. Sometimes it's instant; You look across the room, and butterflies (and other feelings) start. Other times it builds over time—all *Beauty and the Beast* style. You start to spend more and more time with someone, and they start to grow on you. We all have had that one person that started out as just as a friend, and then some moment happens, and they start to become more than just a friend (she didn't shudder when she touched my paw). You don't know why they start to become appealing, but they start giving you the butterflies.

Dating online has kind of killed this process. You judge someone based on one, maybe a few, pictures in a couple of seconds time. Then maybe if you really have the time and desire, you can read the two-paragraph (maybe) profile if they wrote one and make your whole decision about that person on just that. There's a feeling when you are near a person you have chemistry with—almost like electricity between the two of you. They smile, you smile. Body language starts to play a part.

I mean everyone has a type, a general type of person that you are attracted to. It's not exactly your fault; it's just who gives you the wiggles. I'm personally a sucker for tall and blue eyes. Damn, they melt me. Some guys like the booty, etc. It is a nice surprise when someone that doesn't totally fit your type still produces that chemistry. I have been told that I am superficial when it comes to the guys that I date/ choose (I don't agree) but really, I just have a general type that I am attracted to.

I like that I have dated all different types of guys, jobs, backgrounds, income, and personality. You never know. But this damn online thing makes all that harder. There's *one* firefighter that has given me the schoolgirl butterflies for over a decade now. He knows it. I know it. When I see him on scene, I get full stupid and start blushing, I lose all capability of intelligent conversation. He's happily married with a straight, generic, photo-frame insert picture perfect family, so for me, it's just butterflies and eye candy.

Now I generally find myself to be a confident woman, but there are times, especially around guys, that I find attractive, that I turn shy. Ask my best friend what she had to do to get me to talk to guys (tampons may have been thrown). Maybe that's part of my real-life problem. I have a really hard time talking to men. Online gives you a false sense of confidence. I'm okay with sending a million messages, and if they don't respond, it's okay. It would be so much harder to walk up to a guy and be rejected to your face. I have a guy friend, we'll call him "Prince Charming," that I just had a long conversation with. He is that charisma guy. He's not the most devastatingly handsome, but damn, can he get just about any girl. He walks up, smiles, throws out a joke or a compliment, and she's sold. He doesn't use social media of any type. He sees a woman in real life and goes for it. He is very confident in who he is and that helps, but I really don't know if I can be like him.

I don't really want to have to approach every guy that I think is cute and start the interactions. I am a hundred percent old fashioned. I want a guy to come up to me, to open my door, or offer to buy me a drink. I have proven repeatedly that guys don't come up to me; they don't approach me. I can and have sat at a bar or a restaurant and will forever sit there alone. Social media is the only place that I meet guys. I don't want it to be this way. I would love to meet a guy, start a conversation, get some butterflies, and hope he asks for my number. I want to wait until he calls and then hope he asks for a first date.

But all that isn't happening. I don't know what else to do. I have thought about the possibly most amazing or horrible idea ever: asking all the people on my Facebook to set me up on a blind date with a single man they know. I don't know if it's desperate, brave, scary, or genius. I haven't quite gotten to that point now, but I know that social media has destroyed how people meet and interact. If you are a single person in this time, then you should adapt. I don't like it, but I also don't like being single. I can only hope that one of my many first dates will turn into permanent chemistry or that someday I yell at a guy putting his cigarette out on my VIP table, and we end up making out all night. Wait a minute, LOL, or some other version of real-life interactions.

That chemistry is a powerful thing. It's what makes the smiles, and it's what makes you curious about all other possibilities. So for now, I got an A in my college chemistry class, but I might be a C student when it comes to real-life chemistry. Ha-ha maybe I need a tutor!

Cops and Cuddles

How did cuddles become a thing for grown men? I cannot tell you how many times I have been asked over the past few months if I wanted to cuddle. These aren't usually men that I know. It's guys from the online dating sites. Strangers that don't know me from any other person, but they want me to go to their house and cuddle?

Now why is it me that seems to think this is strange? To add to the oddity of this new event, most of the guys that are asking to cuddle have been cops! Now given it has been several departments, but the majority of the cuddle seekers are in law enforcement. Now I am a bit of a risk taker, but these are the issues I can picture. You invite a stranger into your home to, lie down on their bed, and "cuddle." I would assume, as officers, they would have fire arms that the cuddle women could get their hands on, or steal, or become violent. A strange woman could claim all kinds of things or be dirty—so many kinds of dirty.

Do the men really think that we are so naive that it would only be cuddling? At least with Netflix-and-chill, it was a chance that it could just be that—watch a movie on a couch. Cuddling is a very vulnerable thing that is relaxing because you're comfortable with the person you're lying with. Cuddling is lying down together in physical closeness, and when does cuddling ever stop at just cuddling? That's always the way sex starts. Do they think that asking for cuddles is more appealing or polite than saying, "Would you like to come over and have sex?" Do they think that they are being cute by being "vulnerable?"

I understand that we all need/want physical closeness, but even if it was just that, how could you enjoy it with a stranger? What woman is actually falling for this? Is there a woman that is like, "Totally I would love to drive to a stranger's house, go into your bedroom, lie down to cuddle with a stranger, and expect it to go only just that far"? Oh, how relaxing! Give us some credit. Cut the cuddles, coppers!

Serial Dating: I Should Just Stick with Cereal

Now this topic was suggested to me by one of my male friends, and I thought it was interesting. When he suggested it, what I thought he meant and what he did mean were totally different. His words were, "Not fully engaging in someone on the date because they are involved with a few others at the same level. Like 4+ 'relationships.'" Well, I was a little offended. There have been times I have been talking to several guys at a time and going on dates with many of them. I have had to learn how to not totally invest in just one until I kind of see how it all plays out.

Now with my track record, you know none of them did—whop, whop. What my friend was saying though was how men serial date to keep a revolving door of potential sex partners. He said, "It's too easy to slide more toward physical appearance or thoughts of physical intimacy from apps. It's important to get to know more than just, 'Hey, sexy' or 'I bet they are a good f———.'" (He's one of the good guys.) So what he was trying to say was slowly dawning on me; men use online dating like an Uber eats. They scroll through when they have a craving which makes sense why men are so sexually charged online—twenty four seven no matter what they are craving, it's available with a swipe, type, and send.

He talked about both men and women putting forth their sexiest profile pictures to try and catch the eye of those scrolling through. That in general, men online are serial dating for sex. When I am serial dating, I'm trying to play the numbers game to find a decent guy. So I was going over both my kind "the numbers game" and option two, the Japanese sushi restaurant that has the continuous belt of fish for you to feast on (pun intended).

Now if you ask most guys, they are going to tell you that they are one of the good ones. I don't know if I bring out the not-so-good side or they are lying, but I come across those that show less of the good with their actions. I don't go into this at any time, trying to scrape the bottom of the barrel. I am trying to find one of the good ones. That's why I have become a serial dater. I am playing the numbers game. If I go out with enough guys on enough dates, there must be odds in my favor that one will turn out.

Now don't get me wrong; I've written before about meeting some nice guys, and a few turned out to be friends, but I am talking relationships. I've said before that I literally play the numbers when it comes to online dating. I could message or get messages from twenty plus guys; start talking to fifteen; after a day, maybe twelve; after three days, maybe eight; and then more than five days, five guys or less. Then the next step happens, and they ask for my number, and the texting starts. Then maybe three will talk about going out, and two will turn into a date.

In multiple months, not one of the countless dates I have gone on, some have turned into a relationship. I cannot tell you how many dates I have been on in the preceding months. Some weeks I've had two to three dates. Some weeks none. I would say that on average, I would have gone out with maybe three to four guys a month, and in ten months of dating, that's thirty to forty men and dates! If you tried on that many shoes or applied for that many jobs, I would imagine you would find something after that amount of time.

I have a magic block that after two real dates, the "relationship" fails. It just happened again. I met a super amazing man, started dating, had plans for many dates to come (super excited), and as expected, it ended. Now the reasons were because of unforeseen circumstances, but it ended nonetheless. A heavy dose of disappointment was served with that one. He was nice, a gentleman, and everything I had been looking for. All my boxes were checked with him. Yet my curse kicked in. After two amazing dates, he decided he didn't have time for dating or that he didn't have the emotional availability needed to date (part of my curse). Now I can't blame him for this one, but it shows that no matter the numbers I play, *the odds* are never in my favor.

I would say part of that is the men's side and how they approach this process. Like my guy friend said, guys are looking at dating with one goal in mind, and it doesn't start with girlfriend. Guys go into online dating to not really date but to find partners. Maybe they play the numbers games too. If they go on "x" number of dates, one must put out. We are all fishing in the same pond but for very different fish. Now I have seen the woman's side of the dating, and it's a hot mess. These girls are putting pictures out there that a lot of women wouldn't send to their husbands. Ninety percent naked, provocative, and then accompanied with improper suggestions. I think there are women out there that are sexually charged and just looking to have a good time, but what I think more is women have lost their confidence.

Women nowadays think they should show off their bodies and give a BJ on the first date because he bought her a burger. Women need to remember their self-worth. But the trend with that is showing men what to expect. They don't have to put in effort or develop a relationship. They just show up and be charming then onto the next. That is the disconnect, guys seem to always be onto the next, and I'm trying to just find one. That is the divide, the difference, the Venus vs Mars. Women want the *one*, and men want *everyone*.

Ghost Hunting: The New Normal

For those of you lucky enough to not know what "ghosting" is, it's a new trend happening more and more frequently. Ghosting is when you meet someone online, start talking, developing a bond or relationship base, and then *without warning,* just vanishes. *Poof,* like a f——ing magic act. Now you hear from them, now you don't. This can go as low as to having the ghost to block the number, delete social media ties, and to *never be heard from again.* You have no idea if they are hurt in the hospital, dropped their phone in the toilet, died, or worst yet, you've been *ghosted!* Worry and panic set in, and the self-doubt, that gut feeling that something has gone wrong grows and starts to make you sick. Now don't get this confused with cat-fishing; you would have actually talked to this person on the phone, texted, FaceTimed, social media and so on.

A new survey said that over ninety percent of millennials have been ghosted at one point or another. The history of break-ups used to be you had to "man up" and face the person to break up with them, then we moved to a phone call, and then a pathetic text message, and now were on to this. People have now degraded the value of the other person at the other end of the phone. Have we forgotten that people are human? That with dating comes feelings and emotions? The whole point of dating is to build an emotional bond with another human.

So on to me LOL! I met a guy online, and we hit it off. We started talking all day as much as we could. He had just left to go out of town before we started talking, so meeting wasn't a possibility. Phone calls that lasted hours, Snapchats through the day, texting, and FaceTime. We talked about everything from his kids to growing up, food, and travel—no topic was off limits. I got the, "I miss you," "Can't wait to see you," and even a "babe/baby," slipped into conversation. We talked about everything, even feelings. Our literal last conversation was about finally getting to meet when he got home and how we both wanted to meet in person to really see if valid feelings were there. His last words were: "That goes both ways, girl," saying that he was just as worried that I wouldn't like him as much as he liked me. I had no idea that saying good bye to that phone call was the last I would hear.

Then, no response, no call, no answer, and no reason. It's hard to process, to understand, but I have read enough to know that men can change their mind with no great reason, but now they are too much of a *coward* to end it in any facet. Men just know that an unanswered question for a woman is like mental Chinese water torture. All the possibilities of what went wrong will continue to run through our minds like water breaking a rock. I wanted more of these stories to be funny, but dating can be painful. *This* was painful. I talked to him, was vulnerable with him, and saw great potential in him as a person and a man.

So I will end with this, I can tell myself that I am braver than that man. I am his loss. I am a quality woman, and he will miss out due to something he couldn't even communicate, and I will forget about him with time. My pain will fade, but *he* will spend a lifetime without the best woman I know, *me*.

CHAPTER 2

The Leading Men: To Be Fair, Even Freddy Was the Leading Man in His Stories

You, Me, and Your Ex Makes Three

I want to start out by saying, one, this has no reflection on any of my ex-husbands; I get along with all of them, but when I started dating, I was done with that chapter and ready to move on. Two, I would never imagine going onto a "dating website" when I wasn't ready to f——ing date! It's a crazy concept, I know, but it happens more than you know and more than I'd like to know. And so my story begins.

Since I started dating, I have had this plague put upon me. I keep trying to remember when I pissed off some old witch or gypsy that they had to put this shitty curse on me, but maybe I cut them off while driving?

My plague is meeting amazing, sexy, smart, and successful men. We meet, we click, we date, and then the plague sets in. They realize they aren't over their ex and not ready for a relationship. This has now happened more than a dozen times in the months that I have been dating. The problem with this is they seem to like me also, so they don't give up on me either. So the drag along begins.

They call occasionally, text, and tell me they miss me or have been thinking about me, but they have been thinking about her too.

Then they talk to me about her! Now I know the names of several of these women, and I swear, I have never hated a person more who I have never met. These women (I fully realize I only have one side of the story) have ruined these men. They all meet my check-off list requirements, house, career, education, travel, close with family, etc. and with the ones that couldn't quite let go, it seems, I meet theirs too.

Now my relationship with each is different. I did have one guy that decided to go back to his ex after our date, and I never heard from him again. For the rest of the guys, it's pretty much been some form of them tagging me along for months. Some have asked for time, and when I reminded him that we have been doing this for six months, he said, "It's really not that long." Now mind you, some of these guys fit into my "one and done" category, but I've had a few variations. One, a "medical professional," started off talking about being out of a relationship and how "evil" she was to him and his children. How happy he was to meet a woman like me and how we had so much in common. I totally agreed. It's nice to have the fact we both had gone through a breakup in common. I just didn't know I was over mine, and he wasn't.

After hanging out once and with a promise we would again because he "really liked me," he started the talk about the ex. This literally started in September, and to this day when I see him, he talks about how pretty, sexy, blah I am and how many times he's picked up his phone to text me. He just didn't know what to say. Then he starts talking about her, how she was his one love and chemistry, and how she doesn't call him (irony). I tried to be a friend, but these lines are so blurred I just can't. So now I avoid him while trying to be polite. The shitty part is he is super-hot! LOL just kind of crazy about the crazy lady that broke him. He's taken himself off the market for a woman who doesn't want him. Eh, his loss I suppose.

Then my ever so famous Mr. Mechanic. Again, he's got all the check-off boxes. After our first date, he even asked to be exclusive. We (did) have that chemistry; it was just easy with him. But shortly after starting to date came the "I'm not ready." His marriage, separation, and divorce have all been about the same timing as me, but his mind is not. We literally have gone back and forth with dating since *July 2017*. I finally called it quits, again. Hopefully, for the last time. It's hard because I miss him, but I don't think he was ever totally here with me.

Every time I saw him, we'd talk about *her*. It was nice to have someone with so much in common with, but when I found out that he had a girlfriend during one of our longer breaks, his "not ready" went out the window. I don't know why I inspire guys to keep a foot in the ex-pond and a toe in the "Sam" pond. It's horrible and painful. It evokes feelings of not being enough or wondering why they started dating in the first place. For some, I was the first date after the split, and now, I avoid those like quicksand.

I have yet to meet a guy, who after some time and patience, has decided he is now over his ex and ready to pursue a relationship. I should just now know what to expect. If I meet a man fresh out of a relationship, I would prepare myself for meeting a new friend and not a new boyfriend. And of course, I did it again and again.

Last date. We started talking, hit it off, and he asked me to dinner that night. He picked a great place, made reservations, was on time, and when I showed up, had a martini waiting for me (instant points). He was also incredibly good-looking, well-dressed, smart, funny, charming, and successful. We started talking about dating, and he said that I was his second date from starting the app. Okay, but then he said he was only recently split and in the early stages of a divorce. Then if that wasn't enough, at dinner his phone rang, and it said, "[Her name], my love."

If you're not ready to move on from a contact name, you're not ready to move on to dating, and he was not. He was at least honest, and we talked about it, trying to be friends and agreeing to take things a day at a time. I tried to give him that space, but he ultimately decided to try things again with his ex.

It's like a tease from the universe. They are sending me exactly what I want; I just can't have it. So I will continue my search for emotionally unavailable, oh I mean, available men. And if not, I will always have more material to write about.

Dating for Friends

Quite a few months ago now, I started talking a guy on POF. He seemed interesting enough. The more we talked, he quickly told his story that he was recently separated from his wife and that he was at the very beginning stages of a separation. It seemed ugly, and there were so many red flags I felt like I was at a color guard practice. I explained to him that I thought it was a good idea that maybe he didn't try dating right now. He expressed the need to get out and do stuff, to be able to start to feel normal again. I agreed to meet him for a hike the next weekend.

Why, Sam, why? We met, I was hungover and him with asthma and out of shape. Man were we a pair heading up that hill. We were lapped by the young and old alike. But what happened during our

Baton Death March was much more important. I saw in him a person that was going through so much of what I had just gone through. He was living the hell of separation just like I had done twice now. What happened that day wasn't a date. It was "frate." A date to make a friend, and it was the best decision. Mr. Bo became someone very valuable in my life, and I in his. We have helped each other through a tough time, and I know that we always have someone to call and vent to. It's amazing to me that the universe sent out a call for us to come together to help each other through some trying times. Even weirder that the universe used Plenty of Fish.

You see, a lot of people now are putting on dating sites that they are looking for friends and not always more, but that means they are trying to frate (friend/date) each other. I can understand that a lot of people are fresh out of a relationship or busy or have a rough work schedule, that they are looking for new people to hang out with. I blame social media for the new generation's lack of skills to make new friends and socialize. We don't make friends anymore. We don't socialize. We base everything on a swipe and a keyboard. We don't meet people even as friends anymore, so we are relying on dating apps to find dates, friends, and hook-ups. It seems like we have left reality and entered the cyber world to create any type of human interactions and relationships.

I found out from one of the guys at work the other day that there is a new culture of men emerging that is completely going away from the idea of relationships. Their goal is either hook-ups or staying away from women altogether. Apparently, the ones that choose to abstain just dissolve themselves into their work; they become very successful, and that's where they get their happiness. MGTOW or "Men Going Their Own Way," have decided they will no longer be a provider, protector, or inseminator for women any longer (their words).

How have we gone so far from tradition that this is a goal for men now? Apparently, they will use excuses to get out of relationships as quick as possible if they do end up in one. I do believe that men and women can be friends, but how did we end up here? Even more so, what does this mean for the family dynamic in our future? I respect the guys that post this on their profiles. I can respect that we just don't want the same thing, but what about the guys that know they don't want a relationship and still enter with false intention? That's where my screening process needs to improve. I am going to need some serious show of intentions. Maybe Trump can come up with a better vetting process for me.

> Do you like some nuts or big balls really big balls 😜 😆 I've got them in hot bags for you I really mean just for you. I can put my winy in one hole and my bald in the other soft hole
>
> Feb 02 7:46 PM
>
> Just think about it and let me know OK ! No kidding it works out 😌
>
> Feb 02 7:47 PM

The Dude Who Dared Me

Quite often when we are looking for something, we find it in the last place we would expect. Well, this one seems to have worked out that way. Cruising through my usual sites, I came across a cute guy, and we started chatting, all standard. The Dude and I keep talking, and I find out more about him. He is everything I am not. He's younger (cough, quite a bit), he's a stoner, hippy, nerdy, sports guy. He's chill and laid back. He's not a planner, and his motto seems to be, "Day by day." He's got long hair, a beard, and wears clothes I wouldn't pick. He's not worried about having big materialistic things but is content with the simple things in his life.

Now don't get me wrong. There is nothing wrong with any of the things I've described. Different colors make up a vivid world, but if you know me at all, I am none of those things. I don't do "drugs" other than vodka. I am a crazy planner. I'm older, not a hippy, nerd, or a sports fan. We both have said that neither one of us is anything close to our usual date. I usually end up with the "type A" guys. He loves reggae and hates country. It all seems like we wouldn't even exchange numbers. I mean, what's the point?

Then we just kept talking. He was funny. One of the things that really stood out to me was the week he started asking to see me, and I kept having to say no because I was working a ton of extra that week. I felt horrible for having to say no over and over, but he kept asking. He was showing effort that most guys don't. He was trying to work around my schedule to take me out. He was trying so hard to take me to the beach I told him it had been a year since I've gone. He had even found out what I like to drink and got me a bottle of wine and kept trying to whisk me away for a night beach trip with a blanket and a bottle.

Then finally we got to meet, an afternoon dinner date. He wore his "fanciest" shirt, which mean it has buttons, and we started talking. That first date ended up being nine hours long. We started talking and just kept talking. We walked and talked and ate and talked; to say the least, it went very well. He told me at the end he was scared to kiss me and then said "f——it" and did. In that first week, we saw each other four times.

You see, despite of all our differences, he had a lot of the qualities that I am looking for. He was consistent with his communication, honest, funny, and oh-so charming. He had this look that is adorable and mischievous at the same time. He was affectionate and warm. We had no idea where this was going to go; it could be a disaster or a success. We both agreed to ride it out and see where it goes. We both tried to learn from each other and look at the differences as learning experiences and not boundaries. I even found two whole country songs he liked. I also tried to take a page from his book and just relax and enjoy this day by day. All my dating is learning experiences, and this should be no different. This Dude kept asking if I had written about him yet, so here ya go, Dude, a whole happy story just about "The Dude." ;)

Fast forward a few days after writing the initial story, I have said before that consistency is important because it shows a lot; it also shows the first sign of a problem. A few days after I wrote his story, I heard less and less from him. He was saying he didn't feel good, and he was busy with work, but the first day at work, I heard from him all day. Then Thursday night, the awkward text started that he had been "thinking about things." He then said that he wanted to talk to me in person. He said that it wasn't bad and he hadn't made any decisions (insert ominous music here). I kept asking him to just tell me, and he wouldn't. At that point, my gut kicked in and told me what was coming.

The next morning, I ended up being sick and stayed home. He texted saying good morning and asked how I was. I already knew what was coming, and I was sick enough; I just wanted to get it over with. When he was getting off work, I told him to just come by since I was on his way home. That way, it saved him a trip in the future. A little while later, he was at my door, and the super awkward conversation started. I got the classic "It's not you it's me," but he did start off with saying that he "could not understand any reason why I was still single," that I was "an amazing woman with so much going for me." I had asked him on our first date to drop a note in the comment box and let me know why he was breaking up with me if he ever did. He stayed true to his promise there and explained to me why it was over. He told me I deserved to have him do it in person, that I was more than just a text dump or a ghost. The true irony was that he broke it off with me for all the reasons I listed above, everything we already knew, everything we had already talked about.

I don't know why now it was a problem. I felt like we had talked about it several times and had concluded that we were going to ride it out and see what happens, but he took a left turn in our plan. He decided it was all too much, my age (ouch), our differences. He said he was just over thinking things. He wanted to stay friends, but I have friends. I don't go onto dating sites and have dates to make more friends.

To me, "let's be friends" just feels like keeping me on the back burner as a backup option. Guys always want to do that. They never want to just give me up and walk away. They always want to keep a toe in the proverbial "Sam pond." They text every so often to say hi and what's up. Just often enough that I never can really get over them. It's like they have a timer, and just about the time I would be getting over them, they hit me up again.

Especially in this situation, I'm not changing; I'm not turning into a hippy or giving up drinking for smoking. He's not changing, so nothing will be different in the future other than him regretting his decision. If you don't want to be with me now, you don't get to be with me then. I can't do the back and forth. I did that enough with Mr. Mechanic. I've had enough space and clarity now to realize he did me a favor. It probably wouldn't have worked, and he ripped off that Band Aid for the both of us.

Disappointment still loomed. I still saw all the things he said he was going to do and didn't, like the air in my tires or the trip to the beach. The part that got me was from the beginning of talking, he insisted that he was different than other guys, and I told him that I'd bet a dollar and he was the same as all the others. Well, Dude, I'll take my dollar. I respect he ended it in person and that he was trying to do the right thing, but in the end, he went into a relationship not knowing if he was ready for a relationship. He attributed part of the breakup to where he was at in his life and all the mess he had going on.

Men, do not start or search out a relationship if you are not ready. Have your damn ducks in a row before you start something like this. Feelings are real, and it really sucks when they get hurt. So, like all the others this past year, this chapter is not just closed. It's probably "up in smoke."

Ghost from Boyfriend's Past

Just like how Charles Dickens wrote, the ghost from your past always comes back to haunt you. Mine has. They often do. It has happened several times that guys come back after a period of time to reconnect or "just see how you're doing." This one though. This one is hard.

Mr. Mechanic, oh, Mr. M. I've never written a whole story about him, but I have talked about him in several. Lord knows there's enough there to write a miniseries. So here's a glimpse. I started talking to Mr. M early last summer. Due to schedules, we didn't get to meet for a while, so we got a chance to talk. I always enjoyed talking with him, and I was looking forward to actually meeting him. It seemed he had a lot of the check-off boxes that I look for in a man (he really has pretty much all of them). We finally made a date for coffee one night in early July I believe. His schedule is always funny, and so it was later in the evening. We met at a coffee shop, and when he walked in, *damn.*

He was so much more handsome that I had pictured. Totally my type of guy. Those eyes always get me, a gray/blue that's full of mischief. We got coffee and started walking. According to my watch, we ended up walking almost seven miles that night. We walked way longer than the coffee lasted. I'll never forget he was the only man that made me switch positions on the sidewalk so that he was street side and I was further in from the street. I've read or known that this act of chivalry is a protection thing, and he did it without even think-ing. I brought it up to him once, and he said, "Doesn't every guy do that?" No, they don't, Mr. M.

We found out that our marriage, separation, and divorce were all about the same time. We walked until we ran into someone. I knew right away he was chatting the other guy up, and at one point, I thought, *I'd really like my date back.* I didn't want the date to end, and it didn't. We sat outside well into the late hours of the night and almost until the morning. We (I) were freezing, but I never got tired of talking to him and looking at that face. He exudes a confidence and a demeanor of relaxed and funny. He's just comfortable to be around. We sat there so long I was starving to death, so the only other option was Denny's. It was the only thing open at two thirty in the morning.

We went in, and of course, we ordered the same thing. We kept talking, never having the awkward pause. At almost 4:00 a.m., we finally went back to my place. We ran out of options. I didn't want that date to end. We started "dating" after that. He had asked if I was seeing other people, and I was. He said he would be really happy if I didn't and it was just him, and that made me really happy.

Shortly after that came, what always comes. He wasn't ready. The end was there before any momentum even started. That started "*us*" though. The next almost seven months was us making our own pop/country song. I'd call, and he would come over. We would fall into each other without a pause. I would wake up looking at him there, thinking that I would be perfectly happy waking up to that face every day. He made me feel safe. He's handy and manly with his life together. Yet during our time together, he was a huge part of "you, me, and your ex make three." He was always talking about her, his soon to be ex-wife.

He was also around during the summer when I was having a harder time dealing with stuff than I even realized. I was drinking more than I realized, and I would call him almost every time, and he would come. I cried in his lap one night, and I don't even really know why. This went on and on, but we never went out; we never had dates or met friends. It was just him and I. Then after a few weeks or more of separation, he came back and told me that he had started dating someone else, but it was over now.

The idea of him putting his time into another woman, of giving her a title, broke me. It broke my heart. I tried talking to him, and he asked for more time. I couldn't process that since it had been almost six months at this point of us. I was certain I wasn't good enough. I had done something wrong, but in the end, he just didn't want me. In January, we tried to have another conversation, but other than a semi-compliment, it just wasn't even working like it was before. I started calling again to see him, and he started saying no a lot more. At that point, I had to get out, and I did something I never do. I erased his number. I did it because I knew with him, I didn't have self-control.

He's Mr. M. I was falling for him more than I wanted to admit to myself and more than I was ever going to admit to him. That was the last time until a few weeks ago that I talked to him. I saw the number, even erased I know it because my stomach drops a little every time I see it. The playful banter started again. It's one of the things I love and hate most about him. He makes me laugh all the time, laugh till I cry, but trying to get a straight answer out of him is damn near impossible. It's like I'm not worth a genuine conversation with him.

I told him again that I didn't know how he felt about me or what he wanted, but I cared too much about him and if he didn't want me to just walk away. He told me he wanted to talk in person because he was sure that I would "take a screen shot of what he said and blog about it." LOL okay, maybe. I told him I would meet with him, but I didn't believe I would actually see him, and I'll be damned if he wasn't at my door that night. He looked better than ever and still the biggest pain in my ass. He kept saying he wanted to see me and know how I was doing. I can't lie to him. I don't know why I wish I could tell him I don't want to see him, but I can't.

I don't know why he was there the other night really, but he explained the reasons for being distant before, and he was justified in his reasoning. We both are in a different and better place than we were last year. We are both fully divorced with a few crap relationships under our belts since then. Life, time, and space with him is just easy; it's easy to be with him, but I don't know if I ever really was. Other than that first night we haven't dated or gone out or done anything or had a life outside my apartment, but I fall into him like an abyss.

He knows me, the real me, the vulnerable me, and he's seen the worst sides of me, and he still sat there and held me when I was a mess. I sat there and cried on his stupid black T-shirt, and he still came back. I don't know if this ghost will turn into something real this time, but the feelings are real. Waking up and reaching for him is real. My smile with him near is real, but my desire for more is real.

I am in a better place and with that comes the fact I know I want more. I want a real relationship with a real man. I am by no means a fortune teller, so I have no idea what our future holds, but if I had a choice, he would be a part of it. He would be my best friend if it wasn't for the fact I could never settle for just that.

The Hopscotch Champion of Relationships

We all remember the childhood game of hopscotch where you jump through alternating boxes with one or two feet, turn and repeat. Well, I've figured out that that's how some men approach relationships.

I met a guy, and I started counting my lucky stars! He was everything I had been looking for. He was charming and handsome and polite. He planned dates and pulled out chairs, opened doors, and picked me up. He called and was never inappropriate. Dating was going so well that I asked him to be my date to my birthday party. He was adorable and said he'd be honored, even shopping for a new outfit to wear (I was impressed). He was totally two feet in.

He had impressed me enough that I was going to introduce him to my friends. Between my party and a house warming, he was going to meet a few. Then the day of my party with his bag packed and hair cut the text came, "I can't make it tonight. I'm sorry." No feet in.

Now I was devastated. I *never* have a plus one for events, especially something for me. He had a completely valid excuse. He had a family member in the hospital and went to be with them. I understand that. I do. But after that, he decided with everything going on, he couldn't date right now. I even could understand that. He had just had a death in the family, now a sick family member. But shortly after we started talking again, one foot in.

He started with the missing me and wanting to see me, and of course, I wanted to see him again. So we started again, two feet in. A few dates in and even an invite to dinner with friends, he was a hit. Everyone seemed to really like him, and I know I did. The chemistry was there. I really liked talking to him. It was all good. It seemed like he was both feet in. But then we went back to one foot in.

He had some minor drama with his ex and decided again that with everything that had been going on, he didn't have the time to date now. His family member was better but had "high demands from family" that he "didn't have enough time in the day to do everything asked of him." So again, I was sad but wished him luck, both feet out.

But the talking started again, one foot, three squares. Again, he said he missed me, that he was trying to get everything under control so we could start dating again if I would allow it. Well hell, I'm a sucker, okay. So talking every day, all day, one foot. But I told him to handle his stuff, take his time, and then when he was ready, come back. The timing seemed to work since I was going to be busy with work and then Vegas, so it was "plenty of time" for him to get everything done and us to be able to date again (his words).

We talked the whole time I was in Vegas, FaceTime, text, and calls. He said he missed me, wished he was there, and couldn't wait to see me, two feet in. We had plans to have dinner when I got back. Sunday morning, I get my "good morning" text and pic, a happy Easter message, and we talk the whole way home, including about dinner time. Yeah, the dude was two feet in. An hour before I was home, he texted he was excited I was almost home. He was done with work and heading home. And then he *ghosted*.

No reply, no answer, no text, no calls, nothing. No dinner, no date, and no response, two feet out. Nothing until the next morning. I, being "naive" as I can be, was worried something bad had happened to him. Nope, he was alive and well, and I got, "It's not you. It's me. I'm the asshole, and I am out. Sorry to have strung you along," more than two feet out.

I managed to play an entire game of emotional/relationship hopscotch with a forty-one-year-old man. This isn't the first or last guy that I am sure this will happen with. I have an entire two-year dating history of guys switching from one foot to two to none with me—wanting to date, then friends, then talk, then date, then ghost.

This reminded me of a lesson, one I already knew, "Fool me once, shame on you. Fool me twice, shame on me." Three times and I'm just an idiot. I am too nice. I am worth the effort for someone to be two feet in. The irony to all this is he knew about my writing and had read some. He apologized many times for the way I had been treated by other men but always joked that he didn't want to be one of the bad guys in it. Well, just as he feared, not only did he make it in, but he got a whole one just about him. So to my "hopscotch partner," I thank you for a lesson learned. A new topic to destroy my writer's block and inspire me to write again.

A Wristband for Bad Behavior a Three-day Pass to Be a Dick

I have talked about Texas a lot. It was one of those random chances. Started talking through an app, and he caught me chilling on the couch and convince me to go meet him. He was out here on business, and I had nothing better to do than a Bond marathon. It was an amazing first date. He was an amazing guy. We went out a couple times, but he had to go back to Texas, and I am here.

We had talked continuously since we had gone out. He had been an amazing friend and even an inspiration and creative input when it comes to the blog. He was a fan even (until this one). So the last time I talked about him was "non-communicato" when we had a misunderstanding about Stagecoach and me breaking the news. We worked it out, got back on the same path, and ended up being very excited about seeing each other there. He never knows where his work is going to take him, and I'm too poor for a plane ticket to Texas.

So we countdown together, and the day comes. It was the first day of Stagecoach, and we were meeting for the first time in I don't know how many months. We texted, we planned, and then we were minutes away. Across the crowd, I saw him (he's tall). I stood on a hay bale yelling "his name" (LOL). He turned and saw me. I jumped off and ran to him. We embraced and kissed and pretty much didn't stop kissing. A lot of serious squeezes and hugs happening. My heart was warm. This wonderful man was actually here. He told me he missed me, and I told him I missed him too, a lot. I didn't even know who was playing anymore; the world faded away. We were literally surrounded by tens of thousands of people, and it felt like it was just him and I. Tucked deep in his arms, we sat there embracing, kissing, talking, and relishing in the moment that we were finally together again. My lipstick on his face (24-hour kiss proof my ass). My best friend finally told us to get a room. We didn't care who was playing; we just were happy to be there, like magnets finally joined up. We ditched the concert and went for a walk. Hugs, hand holding, and kissing continued, but the talking started.

He told me that he was "falling in love with me, wants me to move to Texas, and that he wants me to have his babies," mind blown. I knew we cared about each other but not to this point. He talked about me and the boys (my dogs), tempting me with closet space and a big backyard for the boys. Telling me he has a big house and that every day and every night could be like this with us together. My mind was spinning. I didn't know what to think. Texas had been the only guy in the whole time of dating that had always treated me with respect and has amazing chemistry. We started talking about other stuff, and the time ticked away. We both had to get back. Keith Urban was coming on. So we got a rickshaw and headed back. I even asked him if he wanted to talk about what was said, and he dived in again. He told me that he "was in love with me," that he wanted me to move there and was asking what my apprehensions were? He wanted to know if my apprehensions were because of his age? I told him no. His age had nothing to do with my apprehensions. I would be apprehensive to move in with him if it was Orange County. Living together is a huge thing, and moving out of state is even bigger. We got back to the venue and split ways. I went to my friends and him to his brother. We texted the rest of the night. I was on a high, a very confusing but positive high.

The next morning, I wake up to a text from him saying that he wasn't ready for a baby, that he wasn't in the right point in his life for kids, and he apologized for saying it. Well yeah, I wasn't quite ready to pop out his kid at that exact point either. What he didn't do is change the rest. I asked if we were going to meet up that day, and he said he had to meet with his mom first and then he'd try. I would think that since he was "in love with me" that he would want to spend as much time as possible together. We got back to the venue, and it just happened that his mom was there and was sitting near us. Then I saw him again, walking with his brother over to his mom. I was hoping he'd call me over. I mean he "loves me and wants me to move in with him." Would it be too much to ask to meet his family? He did what he said. Pics with the family and then he started walking toward the beer garden. Okay, so yeah, I was watching, but I was excited to see him again. Sue me!

He walked to the beer stand, got a drink, and then started walking away. He stopped and started talking to a few girls, and for the first time in a long time, I was jealous. I'm almost never jealous. I'm not that kind of woman; it's not my issue, but damn if I wasn't jealous. Then he started walking away. Problem was he wasn't walking in my direction. He was walking away from me! But why?

I hopped up and headed that way. I was waiting to reenact the movie scene from yesterday where we ran to embrace. I was doing my part. I was running and calling out his name. I finally caught up with him, and he turned, but what I got was not the response I got the day before. I got a "oh, hi." He gave me a half-ass hug and a kiss on the cheek. What? I asked him what he was up to, and he said that him and his brother were supposed to go meet people. I told him that our space had plenty of room and that they were all welcome to join us in our spot. Mind you, he was with his brother (whom I had never met before), and he didn't even attempt to introduce me to him. I figured that was just polite manners. He asked if I was going "to be here tomorrow." I stuttered out a "yes," and he turned and walked away.

I could feel my heart crushing, my chin quivering, and the tears building. I walked back to my friends, and by the time I got back, I buried my ugly crying face into my best friend's very confused lap. After a few sobs, she wanted to know what happened. I choked out the story, and her and another girl were off. Apparently to go confront him. The girls rallied and tried to pull me together, patching up my makeup. The guys were trying to tell me it would be okay. But the damage was done. I had never expected this behavior from him which made it hurt even more. Probably lucky for me and him my phone died after that. I tried to enjoy the rest of the night, but it wasn't going to happen. The pain was there; my head was spinning even more. I was so confused. My BFF took me back to camp early, and I went to sleep wondering how twenty-four hours could make such a difference.

Sunday, I didn't hear much from him other than his text that blamed drinking on everything that was said and had happened. He even told me that I was too drunk and that added to it. I reminded him that I didn't say anything that I regretted. The guys in the camp next to us offered to beat the crap out of him after seeing me cry more all morning. I tried my best to "buck up buttercup" and make the best of the rest of my weekend. The texts from him really started Monday morning. A lot of "I'm sorry," "I don't know why I said all that," and "I don't know why I acted that way." He told me that he regretted not spending more time with me over the weekend, and I did too. He said a lot of things, but none were really an explanation for why or why he said those things to begin with. One of the guys with us said that some guys just "get off" on saying that kind of stuff in the moment but never mean it.

My aunt thinks he ditched me the rest of the days because he was trying to find different girls. I mean he had me wrapped around his finger already. I was old news by day two, and we had three there. He said he didn't know. Maybe he did, and he just didn't want to admit the ugly truth.

There have been times I've been unsure why I acted or responded a certain way, but usually with enough self-reflection and honesty, I can come up with why. At the end, I guess it doesn't matter. He's back in Texas. I'm in California, and neither of those facts are going to change. No matter how I felt about him, I really do need a relationship with a person physically present. I mean, hell, I don't even date in Orange County usually. We went from hallmark to disaster, and like I said before, the hardest part was thinking he was the one that wouldn't hurt me. Moral of the story, get salty. It seems like you can't count anyone out for possible heartbreak. Or maybe all my friends that to me seem jaded are right. If you expect to be disappointed, then you won't ever be disappointed.

CHAPTER 3

Pain Doesn't Always
Come with Pleasure

Where Does the Worth Come from and What Is Enough?

General facts: I'm a pretty decent catch. I know I've talked about this a bit before, but I feel like it's pertinent to the topic. I am getting calendar older, but other than that, I'm doing well. I don't look my age. I work, pay my own bills, and take care of my fur babies. I'm educated, clean, organized, and kind. I think I'm a good friend, a hard worker, and I'm funny! I'm a bit cultured and can be a lady along with the mouth of a trucker who can shoot. My cooking is legit, and my baking is amazing. For the most part, I have no drama in my life. I never get angry. I'm up to try anything, and pretty much have fun no matter what I'm doing. I try and put myself together. I could lose a few pounds and go to the gym more, but I can work on that. I am also confident in what I want. I just can't find it.

People understand that there is self-worth, which should be most important, and then there is the worth that we feel is placed on us from others. I'm always that sucker who believes what people say, but then I am blind to their actions not being congruent. There are a few events lately that have placed me in a melancholic state of mind. I'll briefly explain and then tell you where the worth comes in.

A very good man is moving away, and I wanted to get to know him before he left. He's had some rough breaks with women and deserved to be treated well, even if for a short period of time. We talked a bit; he ended up shy (adorable), and we went out. He turned what I thought was a casual meeting turned into a very delightful date. He was handsome and smelled good. He was polite and funny and interesting. Conversation just flowed, and I was surprised about how much we have in common. I really didn't want the date to be over, but I had to work shortly. I had to ask for a kiss good night, and I was very happy I did. I definitely wanted another, but I haven't really seen him again. His move date is approaching, and he'll be gone for-ever. For that I am sad. I wish good things for him. I do. But I guess to me, I thought we could have at least had a good few weeks together.

Then I saw my "one and done" last night after months. My first words after seeing him across the crowd was "Jesus Christ" because there he was (him not Jesus). The exact replica of everything I want in a man. And when he looks at me with those big blue eyes, I believe it all. There's always sparks, enough to keep us away from open oxygen. The way he looks at me, like he's drinking me in. We always meet, and the butterflies start. Then starts the "I missed you. I've thought about you. I'm happy to see you," and I believe him. He's pretty much every check-off box I could think of. He's what I want, but he shouldn't be who I want.

He asked me last night if I would do it again. It was hard to clarify what exactly he was asking, but I said yes because that's my answer to every question with him. Yes, I would date him again, but I also know he hasn't contacted me in months. I've waited months for a man to realize my worth, and he has not. I still see one and done often at work. We still talk and flirt, but I am very grateful I don't have his phone number anymore; men like that take an intelligent thinking, rational woman and turn them into low brain function.

Now what really brought all this on is today is motherf——ing Valentine's Day. Normally I'm all over this mess, cards to everyone, cup-cakes, decorations, acts of love, dinner, and presents. I love showing my love. I want the people in my life to feel appreciated and loved and cared for. But this is my first Valentines alone since 2013, and I don't mean just since my divorce. I mean I am alone, and now I'll explain the worth.

You see, with the two men listed above, I see them as quality men. Smart, funny, successful, sexy, and great dads, all the qualities I admire in a man; both of those men didn't even text me a reply most of the time, let alone initiate conversation. A text can take about five seconds, so that means for all the seconds in all the days and all the weeks, I am not worth five seconds to them. I would fall over dead if I got a good morning or how are you just out of nowhere from either of them. But I wasn't worth a second date, a second try, a second kiss. I'm not worth any amount of effort other than if I'm literally in their personal space. So that is where the separation begins. Why is self-worth and the worth others place on you so different?

I know my worth. My chocolate chip cookies are probably the best, but my worth to them is nonexistent. They have moments. They might respond or tell me I'm beautiful or they want me, but their actions show my worth to them; that is painful. That cuts to the core of how I look at my value. It's wrong, yes, but it's real. When others place value on us, it's so much easier to place value in ourselves. But by actions, I am worthless when it comes to them and countless other men which brings me to this godforsaken holiday.

Like I said before, it's harder because underneath, I really love this holiday, but this one is like blades. I am unworthy of a card, a flower, a chocolate, a date, and an expression of admiration; and this holiday is magnifying that feeling. The joke is it is singles awareness day, and it is because today I feel more alone than ever. I want to be valuable, to be valued. I want to return the feeling of being cared about. I want to be worth someone's effort. Even more so, I want those efforts to be because they just want to make me happy and not to just get in my pants.

I don't know how to change or improve my worth. How do I make myself more valuable to another person? Worthy of their attention and effort? Every dating book I've read (and yes, that's quite a few) has said if he's into you, you'll know it. Men will put in the effort; they will buy flowers even if they think it's a waste. They will have no limit to what they will do when courting a woman they truly want. So again, I must just tell myself if these guys, if any guy really held me in such esteem that I would be worth such effort, then they would, but they don't? So for now, I should bank on my self-worth because my worth from others feels nonexistent.

Since writing this I have come so far. I now know that my worth has no reflection on how others think of me or value me but in how I value myself. That is the only value that matters.

So That One Time I Got Drugged

This one I debated on writing about at all. In the end, it's part of my story. It has affected me, and so it's my story to tell.

So I started talking about this guy in the story "proof of life." He was the second guy I've dated this year. It started out wonderful, maybe a little too wonderful. He was sweet and charming, romantic and endearing. Our first date was adorable. He tried to fix my car then told the waitress it was our first date. He looked at me like I was the most beautiful woman in the world. He would eventually make comments like, "We are going to be the best love story." Our second date was off-roading and shooting with two other couples that were his friends.

He brought me flowers and helped around the house; it was all "too good to be true." Then he told me he had to talk to me about something. He admitted that he was still legally married, but that he had moved out long before and had been renting a room from his friend for months. He told me she was a "junkie" and had a history of heroin use and was currently abusing methadone.

He gave all kinds of proof to back up his story. I have pictures of her methadone bottles and more. He said that he was scared to file for divorce because he thought she would leave the state with their kids. I had met his friends and seen plenty of "proof" pictures, so I agreed to continue the relationship.

McGruff, my lie-sniffing friend, even got involved and started fact checking everything he had been saying. Something always felt off, but like I said in the other story, he was always so quick to have an explanation for everything. He met my friends, and I had met his. We were spending a lot of time together, at least four days a week. It all seemed good.

He had been asking for me to come down and stay at his place for a while. With my schedule, every time I had seen him, he was up in my area. I had a Sunday off coming up, so I agreed to come down Saturday night after work. I taught that Saturday, left work, and headed down to him. It had been a super stressful day at work, and so I asked him to get me a bottle of wine for when I got there. His roommate's girlfriend was a big wine drinker, so I figured it was going to happen anyway.

The plan was to have dinner all together and drinks, maybe play some pool. I got there, and as usual, he was super happy to see me. I was a little stressed from my day, so he poured me a glass and showed me around. His "room" had pretty much no signs that he lived there other than a few clothes on the dresser. There was more evidence of him at my house than this room. We went back down to socialize with the other couple. The people seemed nice, and the girl and I gotten along well. I finished my first glass, and he immediately poured the second. The other couple kept offering me tequila or shots to help relax me from my day. I politely declined since I don't do either. I said I was fine with my wine. I was talking with everyone about my day, hugged him, and that was the last thing I remembered.

I woke up in "his room" in the dark. I was confused and alone. I was still dressed other than my boots. I felt horrible and had to take a second to even realize where I was at. I grabbed my phone that was luckily near me and saw that it was after 2:00 a.m. I got there at 7:00 p.m. That meant almost seven hours had gone by, and I had *zero* recollection of what happened. No memory, not even bits or foggy, just lights out after the second glass. I found the door and started looking around the house. I found the girl and asked her what happened and where "my guy" was. She said that I "got drunk and he put me to bed," but she thought he had been in the room with me. I told her he wasn't, and in my fog, we started looking for him throughout the house. I also started texting and calling him with no response. We found her boyfriend, and he joined the search. They legitimately seemed confused also; he went to look outside and realized his car was gone. The three of us realized my boyfriend was gone, had left me passed out in a room, and had left where he "lived" at some point without anyone realizing it.

I was in shock and still in a fog. They started to try and console me, telling me I was "in a safe space," and they "wanted me to stay, go get some sleep, and we'd sort it out in the morning." These people that I had only met a few times, his friends, started telling me I was "better off (without him)," that "he was really a good guy at heart, he just has a lot going on," "it may not seem like it now, but you really are better off without him. He's got a lot to deal with and sort out right now." I didn't realize it at the time, but they really were trying to tell me something. I just couldn't figure out what it was in my "fog." I didn't feel "drunk," but I knew I didn't feel right or even close to be able to drive the hour home, so I went back up to the dark empty room and went back to sleep until 5:00 a.m.

I got up then, still feeling out of it but slightly more alert. I grabbed my stuff and headed out the dark house to my car. I checked my phone tried to call and text him again, with no response again. I sat in my car at 5:00 a.m. confused beyond belief, then remembered! He had taken a picture of his driver's license with my phone to send to McGruff, so I found it, and there was an address. I punched it into my Google Maps, and it was less than four miles away. I started driving, wishing I would find his car on the side of the road, at a bar, anywhere but this destination. A few minutes later in the very early and cold hours of a February morning, there was his car, parked in his driveway of his house next to his wife's car. Cold as if it had been there for hours because it had.

I was shaking with emotion, nauseated by what I was seeing. It was clear now. He had been "actively" married the whole time. I wanted to bash his windows in, to slash his tires, to ring the doorbell, but I'm not a very good felon, so I did it Sam's way. I pulled out dry erase markers out of my teaching bag and wrote "Liar" all over his car windows. Then I wrote, "Your husband is a liar" on her window. Best I could come up with in my mental state without committing a crime. I took pictures and started my drive home. I cried the whole way home.

A few hours later, a little after seven, he texted me, saying that he had gone there because he wanted to spend time with his kids, and he had slept in his son's bed. He said that we weren't compatible, and he was ending things, and that my "drinking scared him." Now we had drank together plenty of times, but I couldn't figure out what the deal was since I had two glasses. It's not exactly a bragging point, but I can drink two bottles of wine and still be up and functioning, and I don't black out.

It got messy after that. He was arguing with me and arguing with McGruff. He threatened her saying he was going to file harassment charges and a restraining order because she messaged his wife. That would have been a huge mistake since we had a lot of "dirt" on him that he willingly shared.

The wife responded saying, "How do you know so much about me?" To which she answered, "Your husband has been dating my best friend for a month now and was at my house for Super Bowl. He sent me all the information about you, your addiction, and your children, and I have pictures to prove it." All the wife had to say after that was, "Don't attack my character and leave my family alone." *Done.*

More and more came out after all the information proving he had lied. I had been played, and McGruff was right the whole time. The wife upgraded her Facebook to include all new "family" pictures of all of them together, including pics of him with his ring on shortly before I met him. The good part was the story of the museum.

McGruff had already surmised from pictures that the day he was at the museum with his kids, sending me pics of them and him and calling me, he was there with his wife. He literally called and sent pics the whole time he was at the museum then came over as soon as he "dropped off the kids" and stayed with me that night to go to family dinner Super Bowl the next day. After all this went down, I was telling my therapist, and she said she was at the same museum that exact day. I showed her the picture of him and her, and sure as hell, my therapist saw my boyfriend with his wife! If that isn't the universe giving you proof, I don't know what.

It was McGruff who first accused him of drugging me. When she saw me the next day, she said she had never seen me that bad. Then telling my therapist her thought and what I think happened. He made the plans to have me come down, but then the wife wanted him home for some reason. He couldn't cancel, so he slipped something in the second glass, and out I went. He put me to bed thinking I wouldn't wake up until the next morning, and he could sleep at home then come back before anyone woke up. The problem is bypass patients metabolize oral medications faster than usual, so what should have knocked me out for ten plus hours only lasted for seven hours. I woke up, and his plan was ruined, even more so when I showed up at his house. So he blamed it on my "drinking" which was two glasses. I never even laid my hands on the bottle and made his excuses. He probably told the wife some crazy story on that end, and he got to live happily ever after.

I now must live with that fact that someone I cared about did that to me or, at the very least, got me beyond drunk, put me in a room, and left me with strangers unsupervised while he drove home to be with his wife and kids. I was lied to and used and, at worst, drugged so he could keep up his lie. I've had anxiety since, even worse than usual, and I must learn to trust again. I was a trusting, willing victim, and all I can hope is that I scared him enough that he won't ever do that to anyone else. To his friends that stood by and had double dates knowing it was a lie, all a lie, and helped him lie, shame on you. To the man who did what he knows he did, I hope that a man never treats your daughter the way you treated me because karma is a creative bitch.

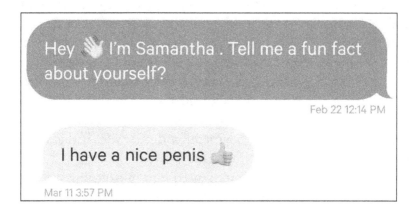

CHAPTER 4

Lessons Learned (The Hard Way)

The Pinocchio Effects

Children start lying at an early age, like it's just a natural part of development. If you ask a little kid early on if they pooped in their diaper, plenty of them will tell you no, but it seems that many of them don't grow out of it. I know that most people lie, just some more than others.

Now I had a conversation about how some people or even occupations have more stigmas than others. I am immersed in EMS; it's who I am and what I do for the past sixteen plus years of my life. In that timespan, I have met a few cops, a few firefighters, and a few of everything else. Men in EMS have horrible reputations to begin with. It seems like cheating comes with a badge (stereotype), but isn't it men with badges or in uniform seem to get more female attention? The job duties of EMS seem to provide a little more of a cover-up for the opportunity to cheat, "Oh sorry, honey. I'm getting held over tonight."

I think that men and women cheat regardless of their occupations; some just get more of the opportunity. I don't know if a ton of bank tellers are getting women passing them their phone numbers along with their direct deposit slips. The old saying goes that "fire is the cheaters, and the cops are the beaters." It's horrible, and I don't agree. My uncle was a cop for over thirty-five years and has never done either. I know many faithful, loyal, and hard-working men in both professions that have never done either. Yet there are the ones that prove the adages true. I personally believe that men cheat because of opportunity, and women cheat because they aren't happy.

Now months ago, I started talking to a guy on Bumble. I found out early on that he was a firefighter, but he worked out of my county, so I allowed this exception. I try to stay away from guys in EMS, and I try even harder to stay away from men that I could possibly run into at work to date. This guy and I seemed to hit it off pretty well. We had a date, and it was good. It was a fun date that lasted way longer than expected because it was fun and easy to talk to him, plus he bought me tacos at 2:00 a.m. He is a younger guy but seemed to have his life together and on the fast track to success. He was driven in his career and education. A few days later, we met up again for lunch, and again, it went well. After that though, he never asked for another date.

I always found it really annoying that I would hear from him all the time, but he would never ask to see me. He always said that he was too busy with work and school and had no free time. Well over the past month or so, it seemed like I was hearing from him more and more, mostly through Snapchat. He would send me snaps maybe fifteen plus times a day, some days more than that. We would have conversations too. Then started the flirty bitmoji snaps, the I miss you, thinking of you, in my dreams, and more. Finally, he was sending the I love you bitmoji, and I called BS. His reply was, "What if I do?" Dude, we've had two dates, and that was months ago. Even I don't believe you love me. I wasn't banking on anything with this guy, don't get me wrong, but it's hard to ignore when you're getting this much "positive" attention from a young, good-looking guy.

Then it happened; I was eating lunch at work scrolling through my Facebook when it suggested this young man as a "person you may know." Well, I sure did, so send friend request I did! Then I clicked on his profile. I never thought to search it out before. Not much on it, high school, college, where he works, and oh, relationship status: "In a Relationship." Hmmmm, okay, maybe it's old. He obviously doesn't post much. But hey, the girl it says he's in a relationship with is still on his friends list. Clicked on her. Her profile picture is him and her standing together, looking really happy, and I suddenly became not very happy.

So it seems that this Hero of the Hose has had a girlfriend the entire time we had been talking, and I would guess that she wouldn't have approved of the pictures that he had sent several times. So I confronted him on it, and he started with, "We are on a break." Well, that's funny we went out in March, and it says that she updated her profile couple picture in February. That's crazy. I've never known a woman to keep a profile pic of the guy she's currently on a break from. Then he moves to "it's complicated." Nope, try again. Either it is or it is not, simple. Then he says, "Well, that's why I've kept my distance." Oh fool, distance is not sending Snapchats every fifteen minutes asking me what I'm doing and telling me about your day and how you're thinking about me.

I admit that I responded in anger because I was angry. He had read my blogs. He knew how men had treated me, and he did it anyway. I told him he was a "basic bitch, and if he snapped me again, I would send his naked ass to his gf." I deleted his Snapchat and erased his number, and I am lucky he took my hint. Far too often, I heard from him while he was on duty and less while he was at home, and that was a big red flag. I was some sort of twisted candy crush for him to play and entertain himself while he was on duty. How messed up is that? I am not a game. I am a human. He knew I had been hurt and did it anyway for his own selfish reasons. I am lucky that it never went further than two dates and one shared Juan Polo chicken.

Have I ever lied? Yes. Am I very good at lying? Nope. That's why I don't lie. I'm not good at all, and I always have known since I was a kid that lying will always get you into more trouble than telling the truth. My dad and my stepmom always told me that no matter what I did, I would get into more trouble if I lied about it than I would for just the action. Lying creates more hurt and more drama. There would almost be no cheating without lying. The pair go hand in hand. Just about any hurtful action you can think of goes right along with lying. My ex lied to me almost every day of our marriage because he never told me he was using drugs; he never asked for help or admitted what he was doing. If he had only told the truth from the beginning, we could have got him help, and maybe we would still be married. Yet he lied, and I'm sure those lies snowballed into bigger and more lies. I can never understand.

Then I met a cop that I was told was a liar and a F-boy from a lot of mutual friends. I didn't find anything that he had lied to me about in the traditional sense. I had given him the benefit of the doubt to prove everyone else wrong, just like I did with the firefighter. It's when people's actions and words don't match up that again the notion of the truth is questioned. I had written in one story that initially, he had started talking to me with the intentions of a "friend-ship" but had called to tell me he was interested in someone else. We continued to talk a lot, and we talked about meeting up. I find it odd that when we are talking, he will say that he doesn't date and that he has no interest in dating, but his goal with the other female was to date her? To me, that's a contradiction of words at minimum. Maybe he's just dancing around the truth; he doesn't want to go on a date with me, but he would with her, "situational truth?"

The difference between the two is that the firefighter started out our whole "relationship" on a lie, and the cop had been, at times, brutally honest, or had he? You see, that's the problem with truth. You don't know if someone is lying to you, not easily. People lie for so many different reasons that you can't always figure it out. So how do we trust?

I will always give each person a chance based on who they are as a person and not what they do for a living, but I'll be damned if more often than not, people prove stereotypes right before they prove them wrong.

Relationship Impersonators

I have come to the realization today that I often engage in inter-actions with men that impersonate a relationship. What I mean by this is that men I meet, when you look from the outside, you would think we were in some kind of relationship, but then, they throw out the friend claim. "Warning! Disclaimer: this man is not emotionally available and will not be engaging in a relationship of any kind or any definition of the word. He will also not be held responsible for his actions hence forth and will not be required to participate in conversations about feelings and commitment. If mention of feelings occurs, please reference the above disclaimer and an automated reply of 'I already told you' will be generated."

We started out talking, and we talked a lot; we even spent time together, maybe a few "dates," but then for some reason, I got the talk that they weren't ready for a relationship for "fill in the blank" reason. Quite often it's that they aren't over an ex or busy with work. Now my question to that is, "Why are they on a dating site or asking women out on dates if they aren't ready to date?"

Now a lot of my answers come from research and writing of other stories. The men are looking for anything other than an actual relationship, a connection but not a relationship. Because of *fear*, they are scared to be hurt or taken advantage of, and therefore if we don't have a defined relationship, we can't get hurt, right? Even the most bitter person can't be mad at having someone to ask how their day was or to talk to when they have a bad day. I understand that people want connections or what they need for fulfillment, but my problem is when it looks like a relationship, acts like a relationship, has the benefits of a relationship but then we aren't calling it a relationship, that isn't fair to the one that wants a relationship (me).

Real-life or online dating, it's the same. Even the times I've met the guys in real life, the process is the same. We meet, I hear from them all the time, we talk, text, laugh, flirt, and even make plans or hang out and then the talk.

They always add in the "we." They "we, we, we" me all day long. "We need to go do this, we need to try, when we go and do…" They throw out those future plans like little breadcrumbs to make sure I follow along like a donkey and a carrot. What it ends up doing is making me feel like an ass because I believe that if they are saying these things, it's because they plan on doing them and keeping me around in their future. The problem is that "we" doesn't ever happen. It's like they are impersonating a relationship without having the commitment of the actual relationship. "We" has become a trigger word for me. Every time it leads to disappointment and failed promises. If they are interested in me enough to talk to me every day about we, then why are they not interested enough to try dating?

The answer: it doesn't have a goddamned thing to do with me; that's all them! It's their fears and apprehensions that keep them from committing. People are bound and determined to carry around their f——ing baggage from one relationship to another. They call it being choosy or protective, but to me, it's making each new person pay the penance from all their past failed relationships.

I met a man that's amazing. He's everything I could want in a partner and in a man. Problem is he's part of the motivation for this blog. He has been so used and abused by all his past relationships that he is completely shut-off to a new one. The problem with that is I'm not them, and I know I wouldn't treat him like that, but he can't see that. He is missing out on a woman who cares about him now because he's so focused on his past that he's missing his present. My opinion on that: start fresh and take chances. Heartbreak sucks, but it doesn't kill us.

Now I will admit that there have been times with this that I am happy it didn't work out, but quite often, it's more frustrating than anything else. It's like I'm some on call girlfriend. I fulfill their need for communication and attention, but they still have the freedom. I am also terrified that this is the new direction men and women are heading, and that's terrifying to the future of relationships in this country. Now I know what you're thinking: cut them off, be done. Well, I am working on all that. I am learning boundaries and learning how to say no and walk away. I apparently need to talk to Trump about coming up with a better vetting process for the men that come into my life. I need to see that everyone is looking for their own fulfillment, and I need to also. If they aren't willing to compromise on what they want, then I won't be either. I want a relationship, not for looks but for real, and I will not settle for less nor will I give them more.

Male Chameleons

If you ask a general opinion of "do people change?" Everyone will have a different opinion. Every parole board makes decisions based just on that, has this person changed for the better? I think the general consensus is that people don't change—a leopard never loses their spots. Or even harsher, once a cheater always a cheater. Yet life events happen. People get older, have kids, responsibilities change, and hopefully lessons are learned.

I just had a conversation with a friend, a friend that I may have written about at one time. Now I am first to admit that often, when I write, it's from a place of emotion. I have an event happen, and I am writing my experience and my feelings about it. He had mentioned that I was harsh in what I had written about him. I felt bad because that time

I was talking to him, he was being a good friend to me and giving me advice to protect me. I don't even remember exactly what I said about him, but now there is nothing bad I could say about this man. The reasons why things didn't work out with us are clear now: he was saving me from himself (his opinion). He saw nothing but heartache in my future if we explored a relationship, and he took the hard road and ended stuff before it began. I have been lucky enough to have a few guys take that road. They try and spare me the heartache before it starts. A little break now is better than a bigger break later. I am lucky to have him as a friend even though I give him more credit than he gives himself.

Another has popped up lately too, as so often they do. Mr. Hopscotch has jumped back into the picture, and I don't fully know why, but I'll take an apology any time I can get it. I have been asking him some hard questions, like why he left and why so many times. I don't always like the answers, but it's all for the learning. I just told someone that all experience is learning, and if we take it, then we grow from it. It's not often that you can have a civil conversation with an ex about what went wrong.

He started with me again, but intentions weren't always clear. Is he being friendly? Is he trying to reconnect? Is he trying to hook up? Or has Mr. Hopscotch learned how to jump in and stay in? Has he changed from the guy that I got to know?

Part of my problem is that I am far too often transparent in who I am and what I want, but the intentions of the men in my life (or the world) are often unknown. I hate being the person that assumes that all men have dishonorable intentions with all their actions.

A guy popped up in my life, unexpected who added me on social media. We had met in person once and now friended on social media. My initial thoughts were that he was reaching out to get to know me and to create an opportunity to ask me out, so we start talking. He was very open when he was talking about a lot of things like feelings, wishes, and being hurt. We seemed to have a lot in common, especially when it came to relationships, but it wasn't advancing. He wasn't giving me his number or asking for mine. He also had said he didn't have weekend plans but hadn't asked me out.

I thought it had been clear that I was interested in him. But then a few days later, I got a message that he needed to talk to me and wanted to do it on the phone. *Nerves!* He called and had probably given me the most awkward conversation in a long time. He explained to me that he reached out to be friends and that there was another woman that he had already been interested in. He had said that even though he thought I was a cool chick, he didn't think it was fair for me not to be clear on his intentions. That was the reason he hadn't asked me out or given me his number. Now no one wants to hear that "he's just not that into you," but hey, I'd rather know.

During the time of getting to know him, I asked around about him, and boy did he get a bad reputation! I couldn't understand though that this guy that called me on the phone to make sure I understood the situation and was so considerate was the guy that had such a bad reputation with women. He had to hear my voice as he was telling me he was interested in someone else, and I know that couldn't have been easy because he said he was waiting for me to MF him up and down. He could have lied, he could have dated both of us, he could have just ignored me, or he could have tried to f-boy me like his reputation would lead me to believe.

Can men change? Is it a facade, a rouse, straight lies? To me, it takes so much more effort to lie than to just tell the truth. I maintained a conversation and friendship with him and, at one point, talked to him often. I told him that I have ruined many potential relationships by asking if this was going somewhere or not. I feel like I am too old to waste time and not know where something is going to go. So I appreciate that he made that call, and I know it was not easy. Maybe he wasn't the playboy he used to be, maybe he was. Unfortunately, things like that are always shown with time. The true saying is that "True colors will always be shown with time."

> ## You are so much hotter than my wife
>
> Feb 20 5:48 PM

CHAPTER 5

The Detox Chronicles

Dating Detox: Week One

Our world is filled with toxins now. It's in our food, water, environment, and even the air we breathe, but toxicity is more than a chemical; it can also be a situation. We have all read that we are supposed to cut out toxic people in our life, and for the most part, I have been able to do that, but what about behaviors? I have started my own detox, and it has nothing to do with a colon cleanse, but it does involve assholes.

The Beginning

One week ago, today I decided to go on a dating detox. I had the most bullshit week of men culminating into this decision. I had one guy that decided to "ghost" me after he said he wouldn't do that. Another guy whom I found out had a girlfriend the whole time we were talking, including the two dates we went on. One ex from the past that has been contacting me, asking to be friends and hang out. Another nice guy tells me he could tell I wasn't as interested and politely backed away, and another, who after planning two dates for the week because he wanted to see me and spend time with me, abruptly ended things two hours before that date. That's one week, folks! It would be a lot for even the most stoic of women to handle. I was a wreck. Let's not talk about the amount of wine and ice cream that gave their life to my stupor this week. To make it even better, the one who broke up with me has been the one that has called and texted every day because he decided we were going to be friends whether or not I wanted to.

There is no one that wouldn't agree with the fact I have had a very rough go at dating over the past two years, but damn if I haven't tried! At the end of all that happening, as I started pulling my psyche back together, I knew I needed a break. Now don't get me wrong. I don't necessarily want to take a break, but I could not be more frustrated that the same thing keeps happening over and over. No one can quite put their finger on the problem though there are tons of speculation on what I am doing wrong (rarely ever what the guys are doing wrong). Some people have been telling me I need to switch to paid sites, but as I have been reading the recounts of another girlfriend that's going through online dating, I feel maybe even that isn't much better.

A lady I know is on Match and eHarmony and her short daily updates parallel mine in absurdity. I'm not ruling out the paid sites, but I don't know a lot of guys in their late thirties and early forties that are paying for dating sites. I am not ruling out the possibility of trying it, and Lord knows it would give more material for this. But for now, I think I need a break.

It's amazing that even me who's not dating still has stuff to write about. So I take my retreat with no real plan or timetable (I was toying with a month) and say *no* to dating. Just like any detox, the first week is probably the hardest. I turned off my plenty of fish and then deleted my whole dating box on my phone. Tinder, Bumble, and POF have all been deleted off my phone, so I can't even cheat. I didn't know what to do with my time at first. I knew but didn't realize how much time and effort I put into dating. I checked those apps more than multiple times a day and would swipe or message pretty much every day. But even in a week, I realized what I got out of this dating thing: it was human contact and attention.

You can talk to another person at any time of any day. You just open it up and start chatting with people that have interest in you. I have had times when I've been up at 4:00 a.m., and I will have guys message me then. I was never alone because I always had someone to talk to. Plus, the attention was nice. I had times that I was juggling twelve conversations at a time. I would open up POF and have ten plus messages waiting from men that wanted to talk to me. Compliments almost always came with these, now don't get me wrong I didn't believe all of them but still the notion is nice. By not talking to all these guys there was a profound silence.

There was only so much on all the other social media to occupy my time. I plowed through several seasons of TV shows and finished two books this week. It is now day seven, and I think that my "cravings" are getting better. I had a few guys ask me to do stuff, and I told them I appreciated the thought but I was taking time off from dating, even when they said it was just a "friendly" meetup. Now the notion of "being friends" with a man should be reevaluated. I generally think that men and women cannot be friends—one person usually has more feelings than the other. Quite often I find that people are not honest with their true intentions. I told the guy that wants to be friends that I wanted a relationship that's why we couldn't be friends. I had also told him that if he wanted to hang out, I would always hope that it would turn into more. That is as honest as I can be. I am willing to take this journey to find where it may lead me. Dating is an adventure, and maybe not dating will be just as much an adventure. More to come as this saga continues.

Dating Detox: Week Two

There is nothing easy about detoxing from anything, sugar, booze, drugs, carbs, and even dating. The first week was hardest, harder than I expected. I couldn't tell you how many times I reached for my phone to check the dating apps. I am very happy that I made the choice to not only pause the apps but to also delete them off my phone. I would have cheated. Let's be honest. In the two weeks I've been "off dating," I have read a few books, spent time with friends, cleaned, watched shows, got sleep, cooked, worked on bills, and applied for jobs. I have had to adjust to having plenty of extra time (and not plenty of fish) that I had invested into dating and talking to guys. Less and less I am reaching for my phone or looking to the apps for entertainment. It's starting to get out of my system.

Yet true to Sam form, my two weeks of detox wouldn't be complete without man drama. Now I know you're asking, "Sam, how can you have drama if you're not dating?" Well, let me tell you. I had three guys in one day, not even a week that seemed to really do a number on me. Some not on purpose, but all confusing nonetheless.

Mr. Hopscotch. Now I had said a before that he had written me and wanted to meet up to talk about what happened. I am totally open to that because I want to take it as a learning chance, to improve from any mistakes. But he's also talked about hanging out again. I'm not opposed to that idea either, given what is said. I really liked him. He was easy to be with, always respectful, fun dates, actual effort (okay, and super sexy). He's been texting, and I appreciate it, but he hasn't asked to see me yet. Now I understand that people get busy; we all are. But I have been told by more than one guy that if a man wants to see you, he will, plain and simple. He will ask and call and text and keep asking until he gets to see you. He will offer after work or on the weekend or pretty much anytime he can because he wants to see you, because men go after what they want. I forget too often how much men are predatory animals. So as my trusted adviser has said, "Think of him like he's on Mars. Don't ask to see him. Just wait. If he asks to see you with a specific date and time, great. If not, you're pen pals, and that's it." I just get confused with mixed signals. I feel like it's something I don't do and don't enjoy it being done to me. I don't know Mr. Hopscotch's intentions, but what I need to do is just do me and let him start the chase (after my detox of course ;)).

The spicy Italian. Super nice guy with a completely different schedule. We tried for almost two months I think to meet up, and so after a short date, he decided that it maybe wasn't working out. I hadn't talked to him in a few weeks, and suddenly, he sends me a text saying that I had "plenty of quality guys like him to pick from in my life and that my standards were a bit high." I followed up with, "Where is this plethora of men to choose from, and what about my standards that were too high?" Didn't get a good answer about the men, other than him, and that I wanted a guy with a schedule like mine that doesn't have little kids. Basically, he was talking about him and not me in general. I have no problem dating people with kids, big or small, but the problem with him was that he has his kid all the days that I am off. Then with regards to schedules, yes, I would prefer someone with a schedule like mine. That's why I work during the week. It makes it easier to spend time with someone you're dating if you have similar schedules, but it's not an end all for me. He said that I was easy to date. I just needed to be more flexible. Then I had to explain to him that no matter what, I was on the detox, and he agreed to hit me up in a month and see how things were going then. All and all not horrible, but it's not always great to start off with a semi-insult when you're trying to open communication.

The last guy that really did a job. We'll call him Mr. Marketing. Mr. Marketing could really have a whole story to himself, but for now, we will address what happened the other day with a tad bit of history. Now Mr. Marketing and I started talking for dating, ended up going out on one date, and he flaked on all the rest. And then after scheduling two dates for a week, he sent me the "I'm not ready for a relationship" text two hours before our date. After that he wanted to be friends and wasn't taking no for an answer. We even hung out a few more times as friends. I was talking and texting with Mr. Marketing pretty much all day every day. We were starting to build a friendship, but there was stuff that he was doing that I wasn't a fan of in the department of how he treated me and who he is as a person.

Then one day, we were chatting on the phone as usual. Mr. Marketing was all about "helping" me fix my problems. We had been talking about dating and this was the first time that I was opening up to him about other guys and dating, and his answer to my issue was, "You know how to get every guy to want to be with you? Lose weight." Instant *crush*. Literally I couldn't think of anything more insulting than telling me or any woman that she needs to lose weight to get a man to like her.

He kept sending me old pictures of myself saying, "Look how hot you *were*." It was soul crushing. And to add to it, once I was upset, he started blaming me for being upset, saying I was overreacting and he was just being a friend and trying to help me. His words "by telling you to lose weight, I'm just trying to make you more marketable to more men."

If you've read my stuff, you know that I already have enough issues with men and, now adding to my already self-conscience state, my weight. I did lose weight. I lost over a hundred pounds, and I didn't do that for a man. I did it to have a baby. I told him that if a guy doesn't like me now, then he shouldn't like me ten pounds less. That amount doesn't change who I am as a person.

I have friends of over twenty-two years that would never tell me something like that, so why does he think he has the right after two weeks? Plus, how superficial do you have to be to think that ten pounds or losing any weight is the only way to get someone to like you? Or that it's important for them to like you because you're skinnier than you currently are? I understand attraction is important. I want to be attracted to my partner also, but it's not the only factor. I'm looking for quality that is going to last, and we all know that looks don't last. He even said that it would help me get a job if I was better looking (aka skinnier). With some serious thought and reflection and some advice, I have decided not to pursue a friendship with him. I don't want my friends to want to change me.

Part of growing and improving my life is removing negative people. Why would I keep around someone who thinks less of me, who thinks I'm not enough, and who wants to continuously change me and my life? I need support, I need love, and I need acceptance. Plus, I need to stand up for myself. Maybe I do need to lose weight, maybe ten, fifteen, twenty pounds, but that's because I want to, not so some superficial man will like me more. I am an average body type now, and if everything else I have going for me doesn't make up for the fact I'm not a "ten," then f——it. Self-righteous, superficial men aren't my type either.

Week Three and Four

My goal was a month, and I am now literally 2 days away from that, and I had a peak, a plateau, and now a dip. I have grown accustom to not dating, not taking to guys, and no apps. I don't reach for my phone anymore to check the apps. I have broken the umbilical cord between me and the apps, and I can now appreciate that. I don't freak about having service to check my apps or how many I should respond to or balancing twelve different guys and conversations at the same time. It's all gone. I felt like I had reached the peak and gone over the hardest part. I had finally started feeling like dating and men were not my priority. I have kept busy and productive, and it really hasn't been that bad. And then...

So out of nowhere, came a guy, a man, a complication. I haven't cheated really. I just made an exception. A guy started popping up on my Snapchat, commenting on some of my snaps, and then messaging me. He kept complimenting me, telling me I was beautiful or looked pretty or my eyes were pretty. Then I finally asked him where he came from. He told me that we had started talking on plenty of fish a while ago and somehow popped up on Snapchat. We must have exchanged information at some point because both of us had some information in our phone. Then last week, he started messaging more, and last Thursday, he watched my crazy snap story about my crazy day and kept commenting. Then he asked if he could give me his phone number.

I had to debate. I knew I had been on detox and talking to a man romantically would violate my guidelines to my detox. Again, I had to think that maybe this is a nice guy. He hadn't sent a dick pic or said anything grotesque, and so I offered my number instead. I have again decided that men need to show initiative, and giving my number instead of taking his put communication on him. Lo and behold, he texted me shortly after giving him my number. We started chatting, and then something shocking happened. He said, "I hate to do this over text, but would you do me the honor of allowing me to take you on a date?" How the hell could I say no to that? I said yes. After comparing schedules, he asked me out for the next day. No weeks and months of texting and going back and forth, literally a date the next day. We texted and talked. I started to get to know him and all with no great idea of what he looked like. Other than thirty-five and six feet, I didn't have a great idea, but man was I pleasantly surprised twenty-four plus hours later.

I showed up to a date to find a wonderfully sexy man who was seemingly amazing in every way. He was funny and smart and family oriented. He was hard working and easy going, handy and cool. He seemed like he would be a perfect fit with my friends and a perfect refreshing fit for me. The picture-perfect date lasted five hours, and there was no way I wanted it to stop. I would have stayed in that parking lot talking to him all night just so he wouldn't leave. Hugging him seemed like a puzzle piece fit. He told me he was raised to not kiss on the first date, and it didn't happen even though I'm pretty sure both of us really wanted to. We even texted on his way home and when he got home.

But then not much the next seven days. Again, it's a guy with kids, and those kids come first, will always come first. That's the way it should be. Maybe he was hyper-focused on the kids, but then if that was true, I would have hoped that maybe after they were asleep or after he dropped them off, I would hear more. When I did hear from him, he said he got called into work. He's got a demanding job, so again maybe that's it. That week he just kept saying that he was slammed with work and not getting home until late. The problem is I don't know. All I know is I didn't hear much from him over the week, so I don't know what happened. His initial conversations were flirty and sweet with all the fluff that made me very hopeful, and now it's gone.

After all my experiences, I always feel like when the communication changes, so does the relationship. If he's not calling, he's not caring, or like I've said before, if the "good morning" text stops, he's done. I understand jobs and kids, but again like a broken record, I don't know if there is really an excuse for complete lack of communication (or maybe there is?). Of course, again I have no idea where I stood, if he was interested or what was going to come of all this. Or I must accept the fact that I may not always need answers, that I must just let it go and see where the chips fall? Dating is supposed to be about building relationships, and if there is no communication and no face time (as in person, not iPhone), then it's impossible. Relationships are built on communication. If it's not happening, it's not building. So the moral of this story is "I guess I'll just wait and see."

Week four also concluded, and I was shocked how easy it was to make it four weeks without dating apps and dating (mostly). When I reached my four-week mark, I decided that I would continue to keep going with this. What's six weeks when you did four or maybe even eight! I have been able to focus on more and accomplish more with the extra time. I very much have had a lower stress level, but on the flip side, I have been lonely. I have a few more extracurricular activities coming up which will help with occupying my time. I have been more prone to picking up overtime shifts; my account is happy about that. I might decide to ease back into it, but if nothing comes of the guy I talked about above, I still feel like it's my time to use for a better purpose.

If fate and karma is real then, if I have a partner coming my way, I won't need an app to find him. It's about time that a man does some leg work to find me. I'm choosing the Rapunzel approach for at least another two weeks. If fate could bring Flynn Rider to Rapunzel, then my man can find me in a first story apartment.

I'd rather have you soak ur bed sheets after I've made you squirt than write in the sand. More passionate anyways

Lessons Learned from Detox: To Speak or Not to Speak, That Is the Question

So I am still on detox or back to my detox? I'm on week six or seven, and it amazes me that once again, I can have drama without really dating. During this week, I realized a few things, and that was my inspiration for this one. I literally wanted to get to my computer ASAP when the idea really came.

So before I start about what I learned, I should tell you my day yesterday. So I was talented enough to basically tell off three guys in about five minutes.

Guy one: Mr. Hopscotch. He's been poking around now for about two months, texting, talking about hanging out, spending time together; but every time I bring up an actual date, he is *busy*. Mr. H has a very bad case of the busies right now (even though he goes to the gym twice a day). So I've pretty much let go any idea of us not only reconnecting but of pretty much even being friends. It's nice he'll text and say hi or good morning, but I've left it at that, until…

So he offered to come over yesterday (Wednesday), and I agreed. I was looking forward to seeing him, and he said that he wanted to talk in person because so much can get misinterpreted through text, true. So yesterday afternoon, I texted and asked if we were still on track for later. His reply, "I forgot." Let me tell you it doesn't feel good to be forgotten about. Now I will give him when he said he got distracted with an issue that came up with his kid and ex, but regardless, he forgot about me, and he was canceling again. You see, him canceling was the major issue for me when we were dating, and now he's doing it again. So I'm done with that one. How many times can I be insane and expect something different from a person that gives me the same every time. I can see now that he's approached that midlife thing. He's having a good time, and dating isn't his priority. And that's perfectly fine but don't lead me on in the process.

Guy two, the guy I talked about in the last part became my typical story. We had an amazing first date, and then he got a serious case of the busies, like bad. I started to feel like he had an automated text response every time I texted him: "Hey, sorry I'm at work, and I've been working eighteen-plus-hour days." I understand being busy at work for a few days, but that has turned into two weeks of him repeating the same thing. He hasn't initiated communication once in that time, not once asked how my day was or how I was. Just busy over and over. I asked him four days prior if he wanted me to back off and give him some time since he was so busy, and he said no. I was good, and he would try harder.

He had the perfect out at that point. If he wasn't interested, he could have just said, "Yeah, I'll hit you up when I have time," and *boom*, done. After that I sat back and waited, giving him space and time to prove that he was going to try harder. Four days passed, and other than one comment on a Snapchat, I heard nothing from him. Unless you're an astronaut in space, I don't think there is any excuse not to talk to someone you're supposed to be interested in for four days and pretty much two weeks. A "hey, I'm going to be really busy at work, but I just wanted to say good morning" would go a long way; that shows interest but also is a sign of good communication. I'm a busy person too, but my gift and curse is I am always thinking of others, and I want the people in my life to know that I am thinking of them, hence communication. I work in public service and have been working all week close to fourteen hours a day, and my phone still works. Just saying.

Guy three. Now this one is a whatever guy, but it's what he inspired that made him the last here. Some guy I had met on one of the dating apps a while back hit me up on messenger through IG. We have never gone out, and it's been a while since we even talked. So he sends me, "Oh, so you're too cool for me now?" LOL.

My reply was, "I didn't know I was cool to begin with! LOL."

He said, "You don't talk to me any more LOL."

So I told him, "Oh, I just figured if a man was interested, he would make that known."

And his magical response was, "Such a man hater." Okay, well because I expect a man to put effort into me. Am I a man hater?

This is the problem: he expected me for some reason to initiate communication with him. And why? He gave me no inclination that he was interested, made no effort of his own, but expected me to put in the effort to pursue him. Last time I checked, the gazelle doesn't chase the lion, am I right?

What happened to men pursuing what they wanted? Every book I've read talks about men being hunters by nature. They need the chase, the pursuit to feel fulfilled. Most men will hunt and fish and be proud of their accomplishments, but no man is stuffing the bass he bought at Vons to put on his wall. Why? There was no conquest; He didn't earn it. He didn't capture it. No bragging rights there. It didn't really take effort to buy the fish at the store, but if he rode out in his boat, put the line in, and caught it, best believe there will be the proud pic of "look what I did." Even more so, most men don't want a fish that falls in their lap or at least isn't sending that pic to his mom! Yet that's exactly what this man was asking for. That, as the fish, I needed to swim to him and put the hook in my own mouth. Uh, no thanks. So my final response to him was, "I now live that. If a man is interested, he'll make it known by showing effort. If there's no effort on his part, why should I show any on mine?" No response.

Working with a guy the other day, he told me he was a playboy until he found his wife. Once he found her, he was determined to do anything to lock her down. He had found a woman worth his efforts (his words were she was way out of his league), and there was no limit to what he would do to get her to be his. This is what we are forgetting. Men used to pursue (that's a verb BTW) women, and now men have turned into *lazy lions!* Lions are always a good representation. They lie around while the females do all the work and bring them the food. The male lion then eats his fill first then the females and cubs eat after even though they did all the work. Plus, the females don't really need the male for protection anymore. A pack of those bitches can take down an elephant! It seems that the modern American male is now turning into a lion, a super lazy animal that just wants his dinner to fall down and die in front of him so he doesn't have to work for anything.

The second part is that everyone's advice is to always "not say anything, don't text, don't call, just let it be." To me, it's allowing bad behavior to continue without confrontation. So a guy treats me wrong, and I give him the gift of "silence?" Uh, ask any man; they are happy with silence. I feel like I am finally standing up for myself when I speak up, but to some, I guess it comes off as "acting crazy." Well, why does it matter how he perceives me if he's already treating me badly? How can men learn that there are consequences to their actions if they never receive the consequence? Maybe they drown me out, ignore me, chalk it up to another "crazy bitch," but maybe they'll hear me? Even better would be that they hear me and learn that that's not how you treat people and especially not how you treat a woman. If a man treats me right, I will have nothing to say other than, "What can I do for this man that is treating me right?" If he doesn't, my silence is over.

CHAPTER 6

Hollywood Couldn't Make This Up: The Actual Recounts of the Dating Life of Sam

The Irish Date Bombs

So like most of the rest of these stories, it starts with a conversation on an online dating site. Start talking to a guy, seems nice enough, and finds out he is Irish, like imported from Ireland, so that adds an extra amount of interest. We talk a little bit, and he finally asks me out. I didn't have a lot of free time, so I turned down other dates to go out with him. He asked if I wanted to go the Improve to see a comedy show Saturday night. Hey, cool! Something new I haven't done on a date, so I said yes.

We continued to talk through the week. No major red flags other than the fact he said that he did smoke. Eh, not such a big deal. Friday comes, and he says that he looked at the acts and no one good was playing, so he wanted to know if I wanted to hit up the Tilted Kilt. Seems a little cheesy. Irish guy and Irish bar, but again, hey whatever.

Then Saturday morning at 9:00 a.m. he texts me and wakes me up. He asks if we can do a day date as opposed to a night date. Not exactly what I wanted; I had a lot of stuff to do, and this would take up a big chunk of my day, but again I agreed. He would pick me up at 1:00 p.m., and well since he woke me up at 9:00 a.m., I now had plenty of time. He tells me around 11:00 a.m. that he was hopping in the shower and that he would see me soon. So a little before 1:00 p.m., I asked if he was on the way. No response. Then I waited. Fifteen minutes went by and then twenty. I texted again, and nothing. Finally, at 1:30 p.m. I texted and told him if he didn't show by 1:45 p.m., then I am leaving to go run my errands. At 1:42 p.m. he rolled in.

First, the guy was younger than me but looked way older, was dressed in head-to-toe Hollister, and a very dirty car. He apologizes and asks if we can still go out. Then it all keeps going (south). The car smelt like smoke and cheap Axe spray. He tells me that he was late because someone else got in the shower before he could. Hmmm, interesting since he hadn't mentioned having roommates. Then he proceeds to tell me that he is living on a friend's couch right now after getting kicked out of the last "room to rent" that he was staying at. Okay, good to know. He told me that he couldn't call me to tell me he was running late because "it would mess up the GPS." Then he asked my favorite question on a date when they just pick you up: "What do you want to do?"

I don't know how he had a plan for dates yesterday, and now today, he has no clue. I am a planner by nature, and so this is a rough subject for me. Why ask someone on a date if you don't have a plan for a date? So he says, "Why don't we just go downtown and get a drink?" Well, hell. I mean, it's 2:00 p.m. on a Saturday afternoon on our first date, why not a drink? So he offers a local bar as an option, and with my directions, away we go.

We parked and headed in straight to the bar. There was no, "Hey, would you like to grab some lunch first?" Nope, straight to the bartender. Round one: literally within minutes of my Tito's and tonic and his Guinness arriving, he's leaving me at the bar so he could go smoke. At this point, I now see that was my escape route, hindsight. His casual smoking turned into a pack real quick in the next few hours. It was obvious he was just winging this. He tried the you look good, smell good stuff I think to still butter me up from the fact he was over forty minutes late. Then he asked if I wanted to play pool.

Sure, why not. I knew at this point I was over this date and made the decision that I was going to drink my way through it to the best of my ability.

We made it through three rounds of drinks before we finished the first game. We kept playing pool and ordering drinks. I was sending SOS messages through Snapchat. The conversation was okay, nothing exhilarating. I found out that he had a very inconsistent job history, had worked for temp agencies, and had only been at his current job for six months and was thinking about a different one because he was "getting bored." He said he was considering a job in Boston, and I encouraged him to take it, mostly because I wanted him to leave now.

While rounds three, four, five, seven, I don't know, he mentioned that we should go to Vegas *to get married*. Then when a random drunk lady asked who we were, he introduced me as his wife. All wonderful things to do on a *very* first date. Then he wanted to head to another bar, naturally. At this point, I've had enough drinks to roll with it, but I do *ask* for food. We walked over to a restaurant/ bar, and of course, he asked to sit in the bar area. Anyone sees a pattern here? He goes to the bathroom, and I told the waitress that I am on a bad date and to make the drink "really strong." She offered a double since he was paying. I finally ate food. Don't ask me the time. I had no idea. After another round of drinks and a small amount of food, I finally told him that I need to head home. We walked back to the car (which we couldn't find for a while), and *he drove me home.*

Now I understand this was a bad decision on my part since he had been drinking so much. I know I was knackered. He drove me home and told me he wanted to come in. I allowed and offered him the Guinness that I was never going to drink. I made another for myself. We started talking about Ireland, and I just so happened to know more about Irish "history" than he did. It was the one time that we had entertaining conversation or maybe I had just drunk enough.

Speaking of enough, he went to the bathroom, and I went to go lie down. I had hit my limit. I remembered him coming in saying, "Do you want me to stay or should I leave?" I mumbled a response, and he left. The great parts started a few hours later when he started texting and calling me. By the next afternoon, I had seven text messages, three missed calls, and two voicemails. They ranged from, "How was the date for you 1–10?" to "Do you just use lads for their money and have fun onto the next victim?" and the best "You weren't that drunk. I left you and went and had ten more beers." He also added that he had a really great time and would like to see me again. I finally had to tell him that if the date wasn't bad enough that all the text, calls, and voicemails were really on the creepy side. He said that he understood and that he wouldn't contact me again. Apparently that meant until the next day when he asked how my day was going. There was a few more text that I just didn't respond to. Finally after about a week, he really did stop contacting me. The next day I had a hangover and, of course, a whole new story to tell.

Moral of this one: always have an escape plan and f——polite, leave if it's a hot mess. My time is more valuable than his feelings.

Red Room Realness: *Fifty Shades of Freaky*

Disclaimer: the following does contain adult content and is intended for mature readers.

With that being said, this one has been developing for a while. To be fair, I have no judgment on what people get off on as long as everyone is safe, consenting adults, and no animals, have at it. The part that gets me is that strangers are asking me (another stranger) to participate in all kinds of activities. Also, I want it to be known that no, I haven't participated in any of the requested activities nor do I search these people out. They come to me, and I ask questions to clarify what they want me to do and yes, to get material. So sit back and enjoy the fifty levels of freaky that I have encountered the past few months.

So the varying shades of kink have spanned the whole color spectrum, from light pink to smack your ass scarlet. I'll start light and work my way to the red room.

Like I talked about before, guys keep asking to cuddle, and I for damn sure know that is not all they intend to happen. I appreciate them trying to be cute about it, but I know dueling it out for who's being big spoon is not the intention behind the invite.

Then I have the guys who put it out there, in black and white, what they would like to do. These messages are usually the first few they send to me and often without me even responding to them in the first place. Some fine examples include but not limited to: "Want to make your panties wet," "69," "I want to eat your pu——," "Down to chill with me and my bro tonight," "Looking for big fun," "I'd rather have you soak your bedsheets after I've made you squirt more passionate anyways." Then I had a less than charming nineteen-year-old tell me that he has always had a thing for "older women" and wanted me to teach him the ways of the bedroom. He was "Willing to learn. I'm down to do whatever you tell me, babe." He had told me he was a virgin and wanted me to teach him things because his last girlfriend had braces, and it hurt when she tried to give him head. Sadly I had to cut him loose when he offered me gas money to pick him up since he didn't drive.

I've had plenty of guys describe their attributes to me and/or send pictures. Their tongue is long or their, uh, member is *huge* of course. They put all kinds of stuff up in their profile pictures, from implied nudes, dick outlines in underwear or sweats, and even for one guy, a complete picture of him with a death grip on his erection. Yes, that's right. A profile picture of a kung fu death grip on his engorged member, and when I asked why he felt he needed to put that up, he said, "I didn't even know that was up." Totally believed that one. (Insert eye roll here.)

That "member" brings me to the next level, exhibitionists! These guys like to show it off, all of it. I have seen every part of a man from toes, to taint, to titties. Oh, and let's not leave out the video. I've gotten Snapchats and Kik photos and videos of all kinds. Some guys want to uh, FaceTime or Snapchat video, uh, at the same time shall we say? That's where the difference between visual males and females become more apparent. There is one guy, a twenty-nine-year-old that calls himself Batman, that seems to have a problem if his pics are to be believed, he is walking around life with an erection. He has sent me pictures and videos from his car, work, gym, and home, all the same. I'm pretty sure he pretends he's driving a manual in his automatic car (if you get what I'm saying). He also wanted me to help him jerk off and then pee on him. At least he said that in the shower, easier clean up I guess. I've been asked several times if I have wanted to watch guys in the shower. I am always curious: (1) What their picture album on their phone looks like? (2) What kind of waterproof phone they have?

I always love the guys that want to share their jerking off, like any girl ever thought that was super sexy? All I ever think about is that line from "Full Metal Jacket" where he talks about that's his rifle, and there are many like it but that one is his. I feel like men must feel the same way about their penises. There are many like it, but that one is special since it's his, so of course, he must show it off. Thankfully with apps like Kik, Snapchat, and FaceTime all these things are possible.

Then we have the sugar daddy offers. These are the usually older wealthy men who basically want to make a "business arrangement" with a female for various terms. The basis is usually sexual, and I've had offers everywhere from being arm candy and lying by their pool, traveling with them, gifts, and then of course sexual acts. When these guys start talking about paying off student loans, maybe we'll talk! The last one said, "You are hot. You should let a handsome alpha male take care of you. I live in Newport Beach. Let's meet up for drinks." His about me section was straight and to the point, "Look, I'm wealthy. You are hot. We match!" I know true love when I see it.

Now onto some of the more serious guys, the "doms" and the "subs" or dominate and submissive. You would think that the guys more want to be the dominating males, and some do, but more want to be the submissive one. A guy did have an entire list on his profile about what the "subject" was to do in each category and how she had to have permission from "master" for just about everything. The list included accepting any and all punishment deemed necessary by the master for her improvement; I think I will take a hard pass on that one.

The more common is the submissive guys. Many of them say they are in high power jobs and want to play out role reversal in their personal lives. Some have been super polite about the whole thing, letting me choose how far I'd want to take it, and that sex wasn't necessarily included in the situation. They offered to pay me for my time and really just wanted me to berate, insult, and possibly flog them while they kiss my toes. Hey, I could think of worst things, and well have been asked for worse. Of course, I shared the pictures of the guy who asked me if I would ever be interested in making a BJ a two-person job. I had to ask on that one how that was even possible, and oh, did he explain. He added that he wasn't gay; he just enjoyed above average-sized penis being shared with him and another woman. I mean, he did end the message with, "Why end life with regrets." I don't think that will be one of mine but hey.

On to my last chapter for this story, even though I feel like I could go on for a while. So I get a message on Instagram from a guy that said he had seen me on Tinder and wanted to talk to me. He was a Persian man who claimed to be a multimillionaire; he did send me a link to what he said was his company who knows. The better part was he was very much into being a sub, and he was more than willing to pay. Knowing this was going to make delicious writing. I ran with it. He started calling me mistress right away and told me that his "small Jewish prick would never be able to satisfy me." He wanted to know if I would force him to the ATM to take out money to give to me. Well, if he says so! LOL.

Then he started to ask if he could take me to a dance club and watch me dance with a black guy; on the freaky scale, that's not so bad. Of course, the normal sub/dom stuff came up. Would I wear 6' black heels and yell at him how his "tiny Jewish prick could never satisfy me," arm wrestle, you know basics, but that's when the super freaky stuff started. Warning if you are sensitive, don't read past here.

He started asking if I would, in other words, make sweet, sweet love to him with a black penis strap-on or if I would perform oral on a black man while he watched or if he could while I watched. Then he told me he was paying his trainer $500 to perform oral (not in those words) on his personal trainer. We went from dancing to way more real fast. He offered money for other stuff too, like watching me have sex with a man that was well-endowed while he watched. It went far enough that he was sending me pictures, real and fictional, of the things he wanted me to do. Now, I am an open-minded person and even some of those were getting to be a bit much. So sadly, I asked him for an exorbitant amount of money, and he stopped calling, also that, and I told him I was a hundred percent not having sex with his anus. I mean, everyone has to draw a line somewhere.

> Ever sucked a cock with a guy?
>
> It's an intimate thing. Sorry done it with a hot older wife 3 times.
>
> Well you are very attractive.
>
> I may regret this but …. how With a guy?
>
> Sent

Riddle Me This: Batman's Dirty Secret

So I've mentioned "Batman" before in at least one other story. He's twenty-nine, works in a bank, good looking, very muscular, and I met him on one of the sites. We started chatting on Kik, a private message app, and of course, that's when dirty started. Now, Batman is a sexual exhibitionist, he literally gets off on having women watch him, look at him, etc. I'll go into more detail later.

So over the time of talking to him, he's sent me more dick pics than I can count. Don't get me wrong. He started with pics of his face, then shirtless pics, then dick outlines, then full-on rod. Like I said in the other story, I had so many I was convinced he was constantly walking around life with an erection. The comment I made in the other was that his dick was out so often in his car I was sure he thought he was driving a manual. He's asked repeatedly for me to watch him in the shower and wants me to watch him, well, to be frank, jerk off. I kept telling him no and going about my day. Then every so often, he would pop up again and say "hey" and "horny?" Easy to ignore.

So that brings us to that morning. I woke up to a message from him that just said "help." It was just after 6:00 a.m., and I was not quite awake; I responded. I mean, that's my job, answering the call for help (RescueSam). His response started out good, "Good morning, what are you up to? [Smiley face]." I told him I just woke up. And then: "Cool, cool, shower with me? [Winky face]." There were several noes from me and him asking if he could "wave hi" and "shower me." Then he started to try and video chat with me. I didn't answer. He kept saying, "Answer doll and let me say good morning." Then his winky faces turned into his "winky." Was I surprised? No. Annoyed? Yes. It's currently a little after six in the morning, and I have a red rocket staring me in the face. Then three crying faces followed by "help" and "sorry."

So then I asked, "Why do you feel the need to show me when I didn't ask? Does it give you a thrill?" So that's when this story gets interesting. The interview and real answers started. Batman, "Yes— [side wink face]—like a lot."

Me, "I see that. And how do women respond to your exhibition?"

BM, "Most like it to be honest. Honestly, I've done it in the car. I've made it show through my slacks or sweatpants at the store. One time at Walmart, this girl touched it LOL."

So at this part, I tell him I am greatly intrigued by all this. I don't care about seeing his dick, but I want to know why. Plus, I asked him if I could ask him a ton of questions because I was fascinated. He agreed, and my interview began.

You see, going through all this, writing these, I am curious now how the male mind works. By the end of this though, I am questioning if it's male vs female; that's different or more just each person individually. Now I'm not going to transcribe the whole conversation. It's was all day. But I'll give highlights and my review. I also decided to survey many of the men I know and ask their opinions on the things that this man does. I was surprised at all the different answers I got. But I digress, back to the Walmart incident. I believe this really defines my point and his behavior.

So Batman is cruising the isles at his local Walmart in the shirt section where he sees a "MILF" dressed more like a cougar, leggings, see-through shirt, no bra, nipples, you get it.

BM, "Yeah, she seemed naughty LOL forty-five-year-old lady. Perfect person to show my dick too LOL."

Me, "And that gives you a thrill?"

BM, "Yes, IDK why it feels good LOL. She had a nice body LOL. She started flirting with me and got close, and she pretended to look at the shirts, and she reached for it and just touched it through my sweatpants and eventually pulled it out and stroked it for a couple seconds. So hot LOL." So I asked if it went further.

BM, "She ended up going her way though. It didn't go further."

There is a lot in this story. I was so confused about why would he allow it or enjoy it? Why would she? Who would touch a stranger's penis in Walmart and who would allow a stranger to pull theirs out in a Walmart? His next story started like the other in line in a store, but they ended up in the parking lot. According to Batman, she said he had a "nice dick," asked him into her van (uh, *Silence of the Lambs*, anyone?), he went, and she jerked him off. They exchanged numbers, and he saw her two more times, of which she serviced him in different ways both times. Again, I see so many things wrong with all of this. His words were while in line, "I made her see it." Now "made" more sounds like a flasher (or rapie?) than two willing participates. Then why are the women so ready and willing to please this man getting nothing in return? Maybe that's me, but that's not my idea of a good time.

So then the questions started again. "So you have no issues with strangers? Are you afraid of diseases? Where do you meet most of these women? So you have limits to who you show or who you'll participate with?" I feel like he was confused by my questions but answered. BM, "I wear condoms. I don't sleep with just anyone or get sucked without the thin condoms unless I know the person. Just stores and malls. Only women twenty-five-plus." Well, at least he has

76

standards. I did ask if he was afraid of intimacy and his answer was "IDK." He did say he does date. Then I asked if anyone in his life knew what he does, and he said "No, no one." That seemed sad; that he had to hide this from his friends and family. More confusing was that he would let a stranger put his genitalia in their hand or mouth (or God knows where else), but he feels that sex is too intimate and reserves that for special "hot women" I guess.

Now the questions that I asked my guy friends in relation to this one guy are as follows:

1. How far sexually would you go with a stranger?
2. Is there a difference between intercourse and all other sexual acts?
3. Where do you draw the line between the two?
4. Do you get a thrill or enjoy showing your dick? And how willing are you to do that?

Now I got all different answers. One said he had no interest in doing any of those things with a stranger. He needed to get to know someone first. Many said that a hand job was okay, but more than, that would be situation based. Most had an underlying rule of depending on mood or situation. Some, including Batman, said that a lot of it had to do with how "hot" she was, and even Batman said I was hot enough to have sex with. So sweet! One guy said he would do just about anything with a stranger. Another said that if a girl is willing to throw herself at you and do all that, it was major red flags, and even if he wanted to, it would seem like trouble.

All but one said they weren't keen on showing their dick to just anyone, and one said occasionally it gave him a thrill to show off his erection. Then one of the guys compared it to messing around or even having sex on the first date. I told him I thought that was completely different, but maybe that's my way of thinking differently. Which is why I am asking these questions and try and find out what other people are really doing and why.

The Q&A continued all day. He admitted it was an impulse and a drive to do this. He felt compelled to show off his member but often felt guilty after. Yet on the other hand, he said he gets a thrill from being watched and could "cum just from you looking." He asked for "help" several times in our conversation. I don't think he ever really analyzed why he did this. He said he's tried to stop but does it on impulse. His goal isn't even sex; it's being watched and getting that rush. I even asked about porn, and he said he wasn't interested because it was focused around intercourse.

Then of course, he begged to video message me. I feel bad for this man. I truly believe he has issues that are probably deep-rooted, and he needs therapy. I am grateful for this oddly because maybe for the first time in his life, he got to be honest; he had to really look at himself and his behavior. I doubt that our conversation changed his life, but I can hope he was able to at least start a little reflection.

He did message me again after I had asked several deeper questions. I am impressed he does seem like he's trying to be honest and understand why he's doing this. He finally said, "I don't know. I really don't. The only thing I could think of is that I feel it's not good/big enough, and I can't use my dick to its full potential."

It got me thinking: (1) Do dicks have potential that they need to fill? (2) Is his whole issue really boiled down to classic self-esteem issues? Wanting or needing to feel accepted and get approval?

Me, "Do you not feel good enough about yourself?"

BM, "I think that's what it is."

I mean, I'm no therapist here, folks, but I think he just wants attention, affection, and approval and needs to feel wanted because he doesn't feel good enough about himself. Which I am sure that the women offering hand jobs and blowies in Walmart and him have a lot in common. We all have this issue, Batman. None of us feel good enough. We are all looking for those things. I want to feel accepted enough, but I feel like flashing my cookie isn't really going to get me that, so I guess I'm not so bad off.

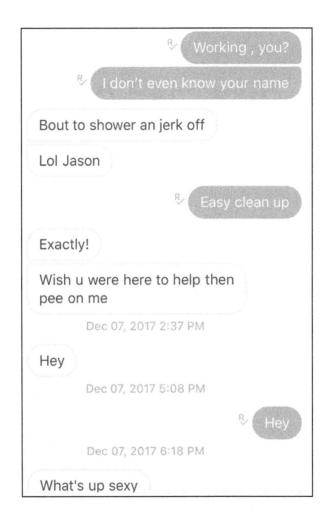

Working , you?

I don't even know your name

Bout to shower an jerk off

Lol Jason

Easy clean up

Exactly!

Wish u were here to help then pee on me

Dec 07, 2017 2:37 PM

Hey

Dec 07, 2017 5:08 PM

Hey

Dec 07, 2017 6:18 PM

What's up sexy

CHAPTER 7

Measurable Growth

Behind on the Learning Curve

How old was I when I started to learn how to date? I was now years old. All this time I could never understand why dating was so much harder for me than for others. If you all have read my other stories, not only do I have bad luck but also it just seems more complicated for me. So now with therapy and insight, I have realized that I had no idea how to date, that I never learned how.

I think that a large part of the building blocks of dating come from our upbringing, and Lord knows I didn't get that. I was never told what I was worth, that I should never settle for less; I didn't know how I should be treated or that if I wasn't treated accordingly that I should walk away and never look back. I have never left a date no matter how horrible it was. I believe that's because I never put my value above someone else. Part of my problem is that I am always trying to fix everything, trying to give more to those who always give less. I have taken the blame for almost every relationship that has failed. I wasn't enough. I didn't do enough. I wasn't enough or sexy enough. It has taken me until now to realize that sometimes it just doesn't work, or that a man could have his own issues, and men do have more than their share of issues.

I just went out with an amazing man, compatible on every level, and the only reason it didn't work out was because of his own issues.

There was nothing I could do or say to make him change his mind because it was his own deep-seeded issues that prevented us from moving forward. I want to save him. I want to convince him to let it go and it could be good, really good, but I can't. He must live with his demons and let his history either prevent him from moving forward or overcome his own mind. I should let that one goes and let the chips lie as they will.

I have had the chance now to finally be able to stand up for myself and to recognize what I am worth and to accept no less. No more games, no more wasting time or making compromises. I am no longer ashamed of what I want and my expectations. I won't settle for less because I deserve more. It's not about female empowerment; it's about self-worth. I am more than a drive-by booty call. I am not Dominoes. I will not deliver. I will delete your number and forget your face if I don't hear from you, and I will no longer accept excuses. Words are useless and action is priceless. I will accept time and effort because that is what I am willing to give, but I will not accept less.

10-80 Pursuit in Progress

One of the best advice I've read is that a man will spend days hunting an animal and proudly put it on their wall. If the same animal laid down at their door and died, they would call animal control.

Men are about the chase. It's not about the animal. If that was true, men would hang roadkill on the wall.

Men are proud of their accomplishments. I don't know if its primal instinct that they feel like they must chase or they just enjoy it. Now there are times that guys take what's "easy," but I think it's because men are getting lazy. Most people will always take a free dinner, but it would get old after a while.

Sometimes I wonder why I am not "chosen" by guys, and I think after this last event, I know why. There has been a guy that's been a topic of the past few stories, and I have been learning a lot because of him. I thought he was interested then told me he was interested in someone else. He had said that he was interested in her first, but talking to her, I found that him and I met and started talking first. He said that there was just something about her that was intriguing, but he also said that he almost never heard from her. Talking to her, she wasn't super interested, and that she just had a lot of other things going on. Then him and I started talking more and more.

Daily I was waking up to good morning texts as soon as he woke up and then talking pretty much until he went to bed. We talked about a lot of things from family to relationships. Then the flirting started; we both even said we had been enjoying it. We talked about meeting up for a drink. I had even specified that it was just as friends. I totally admit that I was interested, but he had said he was interested in someone else. I was willing to be friends, but then we started with the "blurred lines" (thanks, Robin Thicke).

I can't speak for him, but I know that on my side, the idea of keeping it just friends was getting harder. The flirting was happening more, and then he got a case of the "busies" last weekend. The good morning didn't happen, no responses, no communication, so I asked if he was "ghosting." He told me everything was fine and to just breathe. Gave me the "he doesn't date, put the kids first, busy, a lot going on" etc. Being that I am too old to beat around the bush, I flat out asked if I should just stop trying to hang out. He gave me a joke, saying, "Nobody likes a quitter," and that I shouldn't take things personally and that he was a "train wreck" and I was better off without him—that he was essentially saving me from him. I told him that if I didn't want to see him, I wouldn't have asked, but if he didn't want to see me, that was a different story. His answer was, "You're looking way too much into it, Sam." I told him that I was confused (my normal state with men). He told me we could talk about it tomorrow. I told him I didn't know where I stood and that he had a heavy case of mixed signals, and after a final "good night, Sam," that was the last I've heard.

I realize now that I may have started catching his attention, but by being honest and to the point, I killed the chase. After talking to people that he knows, what I kept hearing was that he was all about the chase (10–80 police code for a chase in progress). I don't know how to play the game. I feel like I am too old to play all that. I'd rather know where I stand with someone and not waste my time, but that doesn't work with all men.

I should understand that primal instincts play a role. That's why I write because before I write, I contemplate. I learn from every experience now. I had read that advice years ago and then again months ago, but only until this situation did it really make sense. Part of my problem is I am not a deer running from the hunter; I am the deer asking if I'm good enough to be put on the wall or is he looking for a better catch.

> I'd hide every chair in the world, just so you'd have to sit on my face:)
>
> Jun 07 6:35 PM

When I Grow Up, I Want to Be Skinny

"When I grow up, I want to be skinny, that's what my mommy tells me. When I grow up, I want to have long blond hair, be tan, and dress real pretty so people will like me. When I grow up, I must be skinny and be nice to boys so one will marry me. That's what my mommy tells me." Your parents are your biggest influence growing up. Yet what happens when that influence is a negative one, and you

grow up thinking it's right? You grow up with eating disorders, sui-
cidal tendencies, and a nonexistent self-esteem.

I became aware of my body early in life. My parents divorced
when I was eight. My mother and I moved to Moreno Valley, and
I was alone a lot. All the kids on my street were older than me, and
they "took me in." I was doing things at ten that some people in high
school don't do! There were boys, girls and boys, and girls together.
At thirteen, I was taller than most boys and started "filling out" way
earlier than all the other girls. I envied their small, petite, childlike
figures, not knowing the difference. I was not small or petite and
definitely not childlike anymore. The boys started to notice, and the
clothes started not to fit right. These realities were hard to deal with.
When I look back now, I know I was never fat. I was just a different
body type. My body seemed odd, alien from all the other girls (It
didn't help. My best friend was 5'9" and 125 pounds). Your preteen
and adolescent years are hard enough during school, but then I went
home to even worse problems.

My mother reminded me every day that I was fat, that no one
would ever love me if I wasn't skinny. She was never a small woman,
which is the ironic part when I look back on all this now. The phrase,
"You'll never have a boyfriend if you're not skinny," was a common
occurrence in my house. In fact, that is exactly what it was; it was
a house not a home. "You're not going to eat that, are you?" is a
phrase that triggers a mental Polaroid for me, standing in front of the
fridge or cupboard with my hand on something to eat and then those
words. "My mommy doesn't eat cuz she wants to be skinny, so I'm
not going to eat so I can be skinny." Thoughts of mine as a child were
injected into my mind like poison. Images, events, and words burned
into my mind by my own mother. She made me believe I was wrong
for having the body I did, and I would be punished for it.

The teenage years were the worst for me. At about fifteen, everything in my life plummeted. My friends were still tiny, and I was not.
With everything going wrong in my life, I went to the next level, a
quest for self-destruction. Binge and purge, I became so hungry from
being anorexic that I became bulimic. I would switch between the
two. When I couldn't handle one, the other worked just as well. I

can still feel it—kneeling on the cold linoleum in front of the toilet, toothbrush down my throat, vomiting the only food I had eaten in days. The acid burned my throat; the bitter taste now a memory. The pain in my stomach and throat. I had tears running down my cheeks from the pain or the emotions, probably both.

Reckless partying, drugs, alcohol, no school, they were all pastimes for this fifteen-year-old girl. I wanted to try speed because I heard it worked to make you skinny, but I liked sleeping too much. Then came the pills. I tried killing myself. I don't remember how many times. I figured it wouldn't matter if I were skinny or if I were dead. I figured my mother wouldn't be so disapproving if I were dead. Nothing was going good. I was looked upon differently by my peers for have body that was different, and my mother and I were on two different planets. "I am alone. I am utterly alone," (Beetlejuice) yes, a quote from a silly movie, and yes, a lame saying, but no phrase better described how I felt at that time. My friends couldn't help me; they were skinny. My family wasn't around, so "I was utterly alone."

Life went on, and things got a little better. I got a little older and no longer wanted to die. I then had different demons to deal with. I still had the eating disorders and, as a lasting effect, a very warped self-image. I cried because of how I looked. I tried different clothes and styles to camouflage my body. I hated my body. It didn't matter what anyone said. When I looked in the mirror, I saw a monster. A horrible, obese, cellulite-filled, gross monster; that is what I saw, what I was trained to see. I have kept a journal for a while now and when I started this, I thought of no better research material than what I have already written. This is from less than two years ago.

> It's nice to be around people that you can be yourself around. All I can think about now is my body and how I look. I am reminded every day when I look in the mirror, how disgusting I am. I was joking with Brian on the phone today about me being "hot," and he was just, "Yeah okay, whatever you say." Another reminder. (November 25, 2002)

In the mirror, I did not see my real face or my body, just the monster. And then I grew up. Now that I'm grown up, I have friends that are real (They were always real. I just had a skewed perspective.) with real bodies, little or big. I see different people in the world. I found out it's okay to be different. I started doing hair and makeup. I made people pretty for a living. If I couldn't feel pretty myself, then I could try and make others feel that way. I still don't like my body, but I don't hate it anymore. I realize now how wrong my mother was, and I see what it did to me. It's still hard finding clothes that fit and a date, but I won't die, and I don't want to die if I don't have a boyfriend. I look back and think about everything that happened to me, and I wouldn't change anything because my life has made me who I am.

They say that DNA makes up who we are, but I believe it's every event, memory, and person that has touched our lives. It's taken me a long time now, but I have learned to appreciate our differences because they make us who we are, and I am okay with me now. I end my story with a poem that a friend gave me forever ago, and it's taken me a long time to really read it and understand the meaning.

> Things aren't really as bad as they seem, listen to me I'm your self-esteem. You're not really ugly, and you're not overweight. Think of your good points. Everything you're great. You have a great sense of humor, and you're as smart as can be. Who cares if you're not a perfect size three? You are thoughtful and caring; your actions will show. The heart full of love I already know. Don't listen to others who throw insults your way. Just smile and think of this day. I am saying it now, and I'll say it again, how you look doesn't matter; true beauty is within.

When I grow up, I want to be me and not like my Mommy.

Here I am fourteen, almost fifteen, years later after writing this and I still deal with so many of these demons. You can't escape your past; you must learn to accept what happened to you and to learn from it. I gained and lost weight my entire adult life, and now that I am smaller than I ever was, I still have issues with my body. I have issues with dating and of course issues with my mom.

I have learned that it's okay to walk away from toxic people, and you don't have to live up to any one's standards but your own. I still have beautiful friends of all shapes, sizes, and colors, and by God, I'm grateful for them every day. Yet what I said is true. I didn't write this then or now to gain sympathy but to reflect, to tell my story, and to keep in perspective where I came from and how far I have come to get to where I am. As always, I tell my stories in the hopes that they could bring hope or understanding to at least one other. For someone else to know if they are going through a hard time, that they are not alone, and they can make it through also. Self-love isn't some hippy idea, but it is the beginning and building block of every healthy relationship, including the one you have with yourself.

CHAPTER 8

Recommendations for Use

Battle of the Boys

So it's been suggested to me that I need to write about the nice guys, one, because it probably seems like I haven't had one good date in the past several months, which I have, and two, because hopefully the guys that read this will take away the factors that make a good date or dating experience.

Several of the guys that I have had less than successful dates with, and we're still cool. One guy that told me my butt was too big for his bike has helped me out with car stuff over the past few months. Even the guys that were emotional disasters, I still see some of them, and I can maintain a positive and professional relationship and say hi. I mean hell, I am friendly with both my ex-husbands LOL!

Just because I was disappointed about the turn out of the relationship, doesn't mean I need to hold a grudge and be salty. Most of the guys that ended it, because they weren't over their exes, at least gave me the respect to realize their change of feeling and stopped it before it really started.

I have had some great experiences. I have met some cool guys and had awesome conversations and dates. Guys that were open and honest, vulnerable and interesting made for a pleasant experience. I have laughed and learned things. I have dated guys from all different jobs and backgrounds. I have had some amazing dinners, drinks, and coffee.

Dating is supposed to be fun, and I always try and make sure I do my part to make it fun and look good. I mean if they are going to pay to take me out, I am going to give them better than jeans and a hoodie. I have had dates that started as coffee and ended up talking for so long that we watched the sun rise, and we were still talking. The dates that you never want to end! That date was a cup of coffee, and one of the best I've ever had. There have been fancy dinners, but what the date cost has no impact on how it's going to turn out. I've gone to concerts, gotten a watch, and uncountable drinks, and my ever-faithful Duke's.

The most amazing dates are the ones that time just flies; you walk in and see him at 7:00 p.m., and next thing you know, the waitress is trying to get you to leave because they are closing in twenty minutes. I have walked into a date and a very handsome man had a Lemon Drop Martini waiting for me at the bar! He took the fact that I love vodka and took the liberty of ordering me a drink and having it for me when I walked in. He was worth that new dress, and just because it ultimately didn't work out, it doesn't mean the experience wasn't worth it.

One of the dates I went on was spontaneous. We had chatted during the day. He asked what I was doing (nothing) and wanted to meet in forty minutes. I threw on some more eye shadow, UGGs, jeans, and a jacket and headed to trusty Duke's. I had zero expectations for this date; we had only been chatting a few hours. He was handsome and polite. He stood up when I walked in and was charming and interesting. We laughed and talked, and time flied, and we both didn't care. I was lucky enough to go out with him again, and damn, it if it wasn't even better than the first. He opened doors and picked me up. He took menu suggestions and shared food. He was complimentary but not creepy. He made me comfortable. There were no creepy sexual undertones or the feeling he was looking at me like a piece of meat. He's amazing for being a traditional gentleman, and thank you for being amazing. You know who you are! (Damn, Texas.)

The biggest part of a date is the conversation. You should have a balance, not just talk about yourself but asking questions. When you do, ask questions to make them genuine, like you're trying to get to know the person. It gets old talking about movies, or music, or what you like to do. Yes, those things are important, but there is a lot more to get to know about a person than hobbies. You'll know that the date is going well when you don't have to force yourself to come up with questions. The conversation should just flow.

I was lucky enough to hang out with a guy one night that just so happened to be the last guy I dated before I met my ex. Even though it's been almost exactly five years since I've seen him (I was nervous), it was easy. We talked as if no time had passed. What I thought was going to be awkward turned out to be a very enjoyable evening. ;)

The biggest thing I have learned is that you can't have a lot of expectations when it comes to dating. That's been a hard lesson for me, but once I gave those up, I started to have more fun and enjoy the experience more. Like a guy I was talking to, we started talking about wine, and I told him I like white. Next thing I know he's at Costco grabbing a bottle. Now I couldn't care less if it was four dollars or forty dollars; the point is he asked questions, paid attention, and tried. Really when it comes down to it, *effort* is the magic word with dating. When people put in effort, the outcome is usually positive. I try and look good and be interesting and enjoy the experience.

Guys, when you open doors, offer to pick her up, make sure she gets home safe, ask questions to get to know her, and remember the little things, *she will notice.* That is how you get the smiles and the goodnight kisses (or more). So send that text every morning saying, "Good morning, beautiful," because it shows her you're thinking about her, and it puts you on her mind at the beginning of her day and probably for the rest of it too.

Proof of Life

The term "proof of life" is used in hostage situations when the negotiator requests hard evidence that the hostage is still alive before they pay the ransom. Now I am not experiencing hostage situations, but I do need a form of proof of life—the life these men claim to have. Just in this year, 2019, I have dated two men who turned out to be very married and who claimed to not be. As soon as some digging was done, they bounced and never fessed up to the truth. Another claimed to be over an ex but apparently continued to talk to her. What I need to do (as sad as it seems) is start having these men provide "proof of their lives," the one they claim to be living.

Literally for the first two guys, between my McGruff, the crime dog best friend, and I, we thought we found everything. I am talking proof of degrees, career verification, property titles, and even police and CPS reports from out of state. For the first one, we did a hell of a lot of digging, and the one thing we couldn't find was a divorce record. *Hmmmm*, funny when we found a civil suit with his name.

Now I think our mistake was letting this guy know that we had done the research. When I asked why there was only a house title with his name on it in OC and not in the city he claimed to live in, suddenly he is, "Kids need me, and I don't have the time to commit to dating." Which was interesting since the week before, he was planning our vacation. His exit was a speedy one, and he made sure he blocked me on all his social media, even Snapchat. Now know that I don't have proof he was still married. I just had no proof he wasn't anymore. I would also never knowingly date a married man, but I did get an iPad out of it, so I mean, I guess it was a win.

Now I know you may think that it's "stalker, crazy, intrusive" of me to do this much research into the guy I'm dating, but this isn't the first time this has happened. I have been duped before and wish I would have asked more questions or done more research. I am, by nature, a trusting person. I believe way too much. McGruff, on the other hand, has the convictions of a North Korean justice system; it's probably still not the truth even with bamboo shoots under their nails.

I was only a few weeks into it with this guy. What if it had gone on months or more? What if I got pregnant? I promise you even if I'd like to be famous, it is not through Jerry Springer or any other daytime talk show. People lie. Ironically, it's the truth, especially people you meet online.

My profiles are the truth, but in any app, you can portray yourself out to be any "character" you want to—the loveless victim of an abusive wife, the soul provider for a druggie ex-wife, we stay together for the kids. The sky is the limit and so are the tales. Technology makes supporting the lies possible too. I can tell you for a fact I had a guy text me pics of him and his kids at a museum while he was being such a good dad; then I found out his wife was there the whole time, and people who saw them said they acted like a perfect, happy family, sick. I do this now because I cannot trust people to tell the truth; they have proven that, and frankly, I don't have the time to wait for the truth to come out.

The second guy is a much more complicated case, but for this topic, I'll stick with basics. I told him from the beginning that research would be done, so if he had anything to hide, spill it now. He was so adamant that he was telling the full truth. He took a picture of his driver's license and texted it to my McGruff to make her search easier. He did admit that he was still legally married but had been living out of the house for months, that he hadn't filed for fear of losing the amount of time he gets with his kids or his "ex" going back to the East Coast, believable.

I had met his friends, had double dates as a couple with them, and heard him on the phone talking about being separated from his wife with his family. He was so upfront and "ready" with proof. How could I not believe him, but McGruff didn't. We kept the investigation open, but every time we found more, he always had an explanation at the ready. Until the night I went to "his house."

He invited me over to stay the night for dinner and drinks with his "roommate" and his girlfriend, whom I had met before. The whole night I will explain in another story, but we'll say for now that things didn't add up real quick. I would have gone along with everything probably for a while, but there was so many gaps in the truth that night I had no choice but to fall through. He eventually left me alone in this house, confused and unable to get a hold of him. I remembered he had taken a picture of his license with my phone; one Google Maps and seven minutes later, I was looking at his car in his driveway of his house, next to his wife's car, and that's about how that ended. There was more than enough proof that this guy was messy. It just should have been my choice to end it sooner rather than listen to excuses.

The last guy, it's not as tragic a story. When I met him, there were a lot of pictures of him and a girlfriend on his Facebook. I asked him if he had a girlfriend from the first conversation. He said no, that they had broken up three months prior but remained amicable. I did find out soon though that she still lived with him in their apartment that they shared as "roommates." He swore that enough time had passed and that all his feelings for her were gone. That living together showed him he didn't like her as a person and had no desire to be with her. That the relationship had been strained the entire time, and he never had wanted to be with her (all his words). Once we started dating, she started stalking.

I should have talked to her when she messaged me, but I'm not a messy person, so I told him to handle it. Then apparently, she stalked him on Snapchat, waited and parked next to his car in my parking lot, waiting for him to come out. After that he was "done," he told her she had to move out. They couldn't be friends, and he changed the name on his lease to just him. Problem solved. Weeks went by, and I was finally in a functional, happy relationship.

We spent my birthday together and had a very special day and night in San Diego together. It was perfect! He kissed me good bye the next morning, called me at 4:00 p.m. as usual, then broke up with me via text three hours later. Make sense to you? Yeah, me either. He said he was going back to her and that he realized he still had feelings for her and wanted to work it out. Apparently, he found them between San Diego and Riverside. I feel like maybe if I was that messy girl and I would have had a conversation with her at the beginning, it could have saved me all this.

His wasn't as much a proof story, but I had talked to him several times about his relationship with her, his feelings, and his readiness to commit. He told me he was emotionally available and wanting to pursue a relationship with me. Now whether that was a lie or he was just not aware of his own feelings, I don't know, but it was him living a life that wasn't true.

Every one of these men presented themselves to me one way, but the truth of their lives was something completely different. I don't want to snoop or research. I never want to have to contact a wife and say, "Hey, I've been dating your husband for a month, just thought you should know." I want the truth, the whole truth, and nothing but the truth so that I can make my decisions based on that.

A true relationship can never be built on a lie. None of these relationships were going to succeed, but I didn't know that. I was in them and invested in them like they were because I am living my true self. How can you feel truly loved if the person you are portraying is a fictional character of who you are? So my request for this one: come correct or expect to be found out. The truth always comes out either by fate or by McGruff!

Too Scared to Talk?

Communication is the key or sledgehammer to any relationship. The reason why your best friend is your best friend because that is the person you talk to about anything. Dating is totally based on communication. You meet, you talk, and then you meet to talk more. If you like each other, you keep talking and spending time together to get to know each other. If it's online, then one sends a message, then a reply. Those continue in frequency until numbers are exchanged and the texting starts. That is how you learn about each other.

Communication can build closeness or distance, and it's the one element I totally cannot figure out about men. I don't understand their ideas and patterns with communication. This is where I always feel the biggest disconnect with men. The pattern seems to always be the same. You start out with communication twenty-four seven, and then it slows and stops. It's the MO of all the "ghoster" men. At some point, they just stop with no explanation or reason. They always start out with all day texting and questions, maybe even pictures back and forth. Most will do the "good morning, beautiful" text for usually the first week or so. Then it all stops. Why? All the whys?

People in their thirties don't rely on verbal communication anymore. Communication is all in type (or emoji). We have text, Instagram, Facebook, and Snapchat to help us never use verbal communication. That creates a separation and a space that people can hide in. People don't talk about communication as strange as that sounds. In building a relationship, you should have a basic respect of the others' needs in this department. We can talk about sexual needs, but how much I want to hear from you is taboo?

As I was describing in the beginning, a pattern of communication is usually laid out in the beginning. I usually try and follow suit with what the guy is doing. If he sends good morning every day, then maybe I try and send good night. I try and match the amount and timing of the texting, waiting for him to reply before sending another, trying to find an algorithm if you will for timing of texting and where did this come from? This was never a thing with phone conversations. I have had whole "relationships" with never actually talking to the person on the phone. This verbal disconnect is creating a human disconnect I believe. You can choose to ignore a person and Apple and Android have features to help us do this. What would ghosting be if we didn't have the convenient "block" feature on our contacts?

I had one guy that would almost never reply to a text (using being busy at work as an excuse) but was quick with replies if it was sent through Snapchat, even just texting in the app. Communication takes work. It's effort, and maybe guys have a time limit that they are willing to put in. Or better yet, an attention span for putting in the effort. How do they choose when to respond?

We all know they get it; there's a little numeral one in their message box. I always picture them opening it and then closing without feeling the need to respond. But why? It's 2019, we all have our phones on us twenty-four seven. I even have an Apple watch that shows me all my messages. We are connected all the time to our technology, so why does there seem to be such a big disconnect?

I am a pretty intuitive person, so I know when there is a change in the consistency of communication, it means there's a change in the dynamic. Literally this just happened again. Met a guy a couple of weeks ago, amazing dude, all the boxes checked, but he was fresh out of a relationship.

Now I knew *red flag* for my curse, but I wanted to give it a try. It seemed he was totally on the communication train and even asked for honesty and communication. Done, son. As expected talking daily, hanging out as much as possible, even my favorite "good morning, beautiful" text every day. Then we both went out of town for the weekend. We didn't chat a lot through the weekend, but hey, we were doing our thing. But when Monday came and went without any communication, I knew it was done.

Sure enough, it's Sunday today, and I hadn't heard from him since Wednesday. So I texted him explaining that I thought better of him that if he had a change of heart he could have let me know. Now I know most people's opinions are that I should have deleted his number and never called again, but I wanted him to remember there was a person on the other side of that number. I did get a response, and he told me I was right when I told him he wasn't ready for dating yet (shock). Just like my one-and-done guys, he had tried to convince himself that he was ready for something that he wasn't, and a few dates with me made him realize he wasn't. *My luck.*

What he did do was make me remember something my therapist said, "Maybe it isn't about you." What? The thought that a guy could have his own issues, and it has nothing to do with me or what I did? What a concept! He said that he wasn't handling the transition from being married to single very well, and he was sorry for wasting my time. I appreciate that he apologized and finally responded, but why couldn't he tell me that almost a week ago?

Is it really fear that keeps men from communication? I realize that men are scared that women are going to go "psycho" if they break it off, and for some, it might be true. I have had a dude go crazy on me when I told him it wasn't going to work out, but I was honest. Especially if the issue is with the man and not the girl, the right thing to do is to tell her why. People need closure.

So what women need is consistency with communication, and for the love of God, men, man up and talk. Make any excuse why you're ending it but tell her something.

CHAPTER 9

Change and Not the Good Kind

Permission to Approach

I get told a lot that the problem with my dating life is meeting the guys through dating apps, that it's the "quality of men" that are on the apps that is the problem. That men on dating apps are only there for hook-ups and not for real relationships. I think this is a possibility but not the whole truth. I've met or known plenty of people that met their partner using an app, and they are in happy relationships because of it.

So not that it was on purpose, but the last guy that I dated I had met in person. He was different than what I usually, and I met him in person. All the things everyone suggested, and it still was a huge failure. So I decided to try a little experiment: try to meet a man in person. But how could I make that happen? So just with any experiment, I sat up a hypothesis and tried it out.

One day, I made sure I was dressed cute, hair and makeup on point, and I took myself out to dinner in hopes of catching an eye. I went to a decent restaurant, walked into the bar area, sat at the bar, and ordered a drink. After the drink I ordered, an appetizer, then dinner, then another drink, then dessert, and nothing. Other than a delicious meal, I got no male attention, not a hi, or small talk, no drink or number. I felt full but defeated, thinking, *What am I doing wrong?* I blamed myself at first and then tried to look at the whole picture. As silly as it sounds, I went to my car in the parking lot and filmed a TikTok about what happened. I had described the events and said, "What has happened to men?" I never thought my fifteen-second video would end up with seventy thousand views and over seven hundred comments!

Obviously, the writer in me saw this as a vast ocean of opinions and information. I read every comment, and a lot of them were ideas I never thought of. Maybe they were all married, maybe they wanted to enjoy a quiet meal themselves, maybe they assumed I was waiting for someone, maybe they didn't find me attractive, but the two most repeated reasons the men gave for me not being approached were as follows:

1. Men are tired of rejection which has led them to give up on trying at all.
2. In short, the "Me Too" movement has made men afraid and frankly unwilling to approach women anymore. It was probably close to sixty percent of the comments was men saying that the new women's lib and feminist movements have scared men off being traditional gentlemen. The men said they are afraid to even open a door for a woman anymore for fear of her screaming about her ability to do it herself or law suits for "harassment." They feel that this is the reason for change, and it seems to be increasing in its momentum. A few of the guys said they were tired of being taken advantage of and that they felt they would rather be alone than either risk losing assets in a divorce or a lawsuit for potential harassment. Some were as dramatic to compare saying hi to a woman as possible jail time.

But has this also been an excuse to revive the "lazy lion" mentality that men tend to fall back on. Let the women come to them, make the first move, initiate conversation, because that's "safe." Or have we now conditioned our men to do less because women accept less? Women who accept the "Netflix and chill" version of a date are accepting the loss of opening doors, picking her up, making plans, and putting in that courting effort. She's allowed him to give up on being a gentleman, and she is now accepting him even barely acting as a traditional man. I understand times are changing, and believe me, dating is on that fast track to a complete 360, but I can't be the only woman that is missing the "way it used to be," the act of a man vying for your attention and to earn your affection by the acts of courting. Women were viewed as valued, a prize to be won, and now a potential hazard to be avoided?

So the question is who's to blame for the change? And who is truly happy with how things are changing and the direction it's going in?

> I truly don't need you. I will not buy your dinner, buy you drinks, buy you presents, pretend to be nice even if you are not. We will split the bil. I don't date pet owners. I'm ocd. You will hear it like it is. If you think you are special just because you are woman then swipe left.
> Cheers

Objects of Disappointment

When it comes to fixing anything, I am pretty much useless. I don't do tools or building anything. That's probably a big reason I have never shopped at IKEA. I could never put any of the stuff together. I don't even know if I could honestly change a tire. I admit this: I have strengths and weaknesses just like anyone. I've had to depend on men to help me when it comes to these situations. I'm not proud, but I can be resourceful. I got a bike from work once, and it came in a box. I got two guys from work to put it together in the parking lot one night just so I could have a functioning bike.

When I was single before, I had bought a portable closet. I tried to put it together myself and failed. It started to be this thing after a while that I would tell my dates about it, and they would almost always offer to put it together. I'm sure they all viewed it as a way in and to show off their "manly" abilities and impress me. The joke was: they never did. Date after date and guy after guy would offer to put that bad boy together, and month after month, it stayed half in the box unmade.

I've grown up with disappointment. My mother was the queen of unfulfilled promises. That is exactly where my pet peeve comes from. It drives me *insane* when someone says they are going to do something and then doesn't. I am almost positive it wasn't until my ex-husband that the closet was finally put together. But that damn closet was a representation of disappointment in men and of failed promises. It ended up not being about the closet but about being a "man of your word" and doing what you say you will.

All those guys that offered and didn't showed their character. Don't get me wrong; I have no expectations of anyone. If you don't offer, I don't expect it. Now a new object has arisen, and the same trend is happening. I had Mr. Hopscotch ask if I wanted to go on a date riding bikes at the beach. Uh yeah, super cool date idea! I even have a bike, well, kind of. You see, I got a beach cruiser quite a few years ago and never really used it. The bike has two flat tires, a chain off, and some rust. He said he would be happy to resurrect the bike to working order again. Apparently, this is all easy fixes. I even have the tubes for the tires. So I pulled out the bike and the tubes, bell still works, check, and was ready for prince charming to ride in and fix my trusty steed. To this day, this moment, my trusty steed still has two flat tires. I think I might have fixed the chain? LOL.

But I will continue to wait on men because men have continued to disappoint me. I'm not usually a man-basher, but damn, if I haven't had my fair share of disappointment from the opposite sex. Since Mr. Hopscotch, there have been a few guys to "offer" to fix the bike for me, but now is the time to learn the lesson. I should learn to do stuff myself or at least make enough money to pay a person to fix things for me. I can't depend on people, but more, I can't depend on men. I can only hope that someday a guy will walk into my life and be "different" to be the man that all the other guys never could be. To be the man that shows me again the difference between a man and a guy and renews my faith that there really are good men out there still.

So such is life, it happened again; a nice guy that's been a friend talked about hanging out. He's had relationship problems, and I tried and helped with listening and advised as much as possible because let's be honest, *I get it.* He sits around and gets depressed, always says he needs to go out, so I offered to go and hang out tonight. I even offered to drive to Orange County to hang with him, and *he flakes,* makes excuses about needing to "wash his dog and grocery shop" even though he just said he slept on the beach for two hours.

This isn't a romantic issue; it's me putting myself out there and offering eighty percent and getting nothing back. That is my problem, well one of them; I always give out more than I get. I learned this valuable lesson from therapy. It's why I'm constantly disappointed, I expect men or people in general to be willing to do the things I am willing to do, I will never know. I always am on the eighty twenty relationship plan with most of the people in my life. I, at least, recognize it, and I am finally starting to do something about it. It should never be too much to expect people to meet you halfway and to learn limits. Everything can be a lesson, especially the disappointments.

The Hail Mary

So I was talking to a group of guys about a short but confusing event that had happened the night before. I saw this guy on the dating sites for a while, not my type, but I wanted to try something different, so I swiped right and *boom,* match. He started writing me shortly after. Cute guy in a "public service" job, and we started talking. So far so good; he seemed funny. He told me he lived in OC but worked in the IE and drove by my location every day for work. He mentioned that we should hang out after work someday soon. Sure, why not? I made a witty comment about having a "white undershirt date." Many of us in public service wear white undershirts, and if you're going to something after work, often, you're wearing work pants and that shirt. He agreed and said it sounded like a plan.

I told him I was already there, meaning I was wearing an undershirt and work pants since I was shopping after work. His response (the Hail Mary), "Hmmmmm, sexy. You should do a wet T-shirt contest. I already have the water." Woah, WTF, bro! Where did that play come from? I was so confused.

I responded, "Uhhh, pretty cheeky?"

He responded with, "I'm sorry. I was just being funny." I told him that I understand and that I was a little defensive since guys say some really raunchy things to me and most just wanna bone. And that's when he deleted the conversation. I was confused. Obviously, I gave more credit to the occupation than deserved because according to the guys I was telling this story to, he was throwing out the "Hail Mary" and fishing.

Now don't get me wrong. I have had at least hundreds of conversations go nowhere, so one that ended isn't a big deal. Yeah, I was slightly set aback that we went from "hi" to wet T-shirts in 2.5 seconds, but I am glad it did, so I got to learn this lesson. Men (and women I'm told) throw out the "Hail Mary" early in conversations to see the temperature, if you will, of the person they are talking to. To my understanding, a "Hail Mary" is a risky play that attempts an impossible point gain; it's an all-in or nothing goal.

They make some semi-crude comment and wait for the response. If it's positive, *score*! If it's like mine, they can try and pull off the "just kidding" or just accept they lost the ball and start a new game. The one thing we all have in common is that none of us want to waste time. Obviously, this "gentleman" was looking for something specific, and so he threw out the bait that he thought would attract what he was fishing for.

I now realize that this happens way more than I even knew, and it's okay! Just had another one yesterday—started talking about dinner, he sent me a pic of what he was having, and I sent him one of my baggie of trail mix (wah, wah). Then after, he said that I should come over for dinner and that I could be "dessert." Of course, he followed up with the classic "just kidding." I didn't chastise him for it, no point. He was fishing for something specific, and I wasn't hooked. I appreciate that he's not wasting either one of our time.

So if anyone has a clever response other than my now classic, "Oh," I'd appreciate it. That's the reason I write and the reason why I talk to everyone, to learn these insider trading secrets. I can't tell you if they are helping me, but I am passing along my wisdom, and it seems that I have been able to help others a little, which makes it all worthwhile.

Cause and Effect

While sitting at brunch the other day, sipping on champagne, like I usually do (I wish), my friends and I were talking about my dating life (that we so do). They couldn't understand why a catch like me ;) would have such a problem with dating. Now we have all solidly established that my "picker" is off, meaning most of the time, I'm picking the wrong guys. Even with that, my girlfriend has been trying to hook me up with every single guy she knows, and they have all gone bust! Some of the theory was that it was online guys/dating that was the problem, but alas, no, still a flaming fail. So what is the problem with people in their thirties that makes dating so impossible?

I think it's a cyclical process that has spun out of control. Just like the chicken and the egg, it doesn't matter which came first; the result is the same—people are all fucked up now! At some point, a nice guy dated a girl, she treated him like crap, they broke up, and he turned into an asshole because of how he was treated. Then this newly developed asshole found a nice girl, decided to date her, dicked her over as expected, and then she went all psycho. Then the cycle was perpetuated.

She rolled down the road, found a nice guy to destroy, and here we are today. I do believe that everyone has that person that really did a number on them; then that influenced how they treat others. That was my problem with all the guys I've found hung up on exes. These guys were probably nice guys at some point, and these women did a number on them, so then they do a number on me. My problem is I don't go treating other people like crap because someone treated me bad. I could be that girl, Lord knows I have enough excuses of being treated poorly, but I refuse to treat others badly because of how I was treated.

That's the problem this generation is creating: we blame our behavior on everything but ourselves. We have no accountability; that's why "ghosting" is possible. "My parents spanked me," so I'm a victim; "I watched video games," so I'm violent; "My parents didn't teach me about money," so I'm broke; and last, "My ex really hurt me," so therefore I'm going to hurt everyone else.

I've heard a lot of excuses lately. People giving blame to everyone and everything but themselves. I understand that I'm not perfect, but I can tell you I don't believe I have ever deserved some of the ways I've been treated by countless men in my life. But unfortunately, I am an eternal optimist. I do believe that the possibilities for me are out there. That I could meet an amazing man that's as crazy about me as I am about him. But it comes down to choices. We can choose, he can choose, and she can choose.

So all I can do is try and break the cycle when it comes to me. I will always treat others how I want to be treated and not even how they deserve. I am the woman that will cook for you when you're hungry and text good morning to hopefully make you smile, but I will also learn when someone doesn't deserve my kindness anymore. My cause is my hope, and my effect is how I will treat the people who come into my life.

One and Done

Now the title may invoke a certain picture in your mind, but in my world, there are two different descriptions. We have a new talent arising that is developing and mastering a skill the "Fuk Boys," and then the little more frequent "one-and-done" daters.

I'll start with the one-and-done daters and save the special Fuk Boys for last. The whole point of dating is to determine if you have chemistry with someone and if you want to continue to get to know them. There is a separate part for the casual encounters, the coffee dates, to see if there is chemistry. I mean it's online dating; you should meet up in person to really find if you have a connection with someone. I always feel that if you invest four dollars and an hour into the date and it doesn't work out, I'm okay with that.

The one-and-done daters seem to be my specialty or my luck (FML). These guys are the ones that you talk to, develop some interest, and then get asked out. They start with the sweet talk that you deserve to be treated better than you have: "I don't know how you're single," and they like to talk about the future already. "Well if it keeps going like this, and I'm sure it will, then you'll have to, [come up to my house, go on vacation, etc.]." All the sweet promises to really show their sweet intentions. They always promise that they are different than all the other guys. I've even got to the point where I've told them, "Yeah, well see," to all their nonsense.

You agree to meet up on a date, and you go out. Now this isn't the Starbucks meet up; this is dinner, drinks, and something of quality. The dates always go well—charming conversation, dinner, laughing, a general definition of a successful date. Now I can understand if they were being polite to make it through the evening because at some point, they decided they weren't interested. Totally fair, but this is where the one-and-done daters throw in the wrench; they always ask for a second date before the first date is even over, which usually is polite and flattering, but the second date never comes.

They ask for a second date. Say they can't wait to see you again and usually even kiss you good night after walking you to your car. You will always get a text or a call the next day, but those will all fade away. You will probably never actually see this man again, but you will hear from him again. He'll call occasionally. Say he was thinking about you, wanted to see how you were doing, but never actually make the plans to see you again. I have a few of these boys still in my life. We went out, had a good time, and I never have seen them again. I can't understand for the life of me why.

I hate unanswered questions! I hate not knowing why, but when I do ask the questions, it appears there is a bad case of the busies going around. It's everyone's excuse. Just like I've learned at work, I need to stop asking why because (1) everyone lies; and (2) you probably don't want the real answer anyway.

Now on to the real talent, the Fuk Boys. I think that this isn't a new thing; it's just getting perfected now. Now for a guy to qualify as a fuk boy, they usually are good-looking, but that's not the most important factors. They must be charming as fuck. The smile, the quick wit, the flirting, the subtlety of being ever so slightly vulnerable, but a little bit bad boy mix.

They start with a flirt, a quick compliment, then phone numbers, and then the communication begins. They call, they text, and they even FaceTime! They tell you you're beautiful and that they can't stop thinking about you. They want to see you soon, but they have been so busy. Then comes the hook. They have been wanting to see you, but they are so busy right now so, (ready for the good part) "Why don't you just come over and hang out at my place tonight so we can spend time, and next week we'll go on an actual date?"

So you think, "Yeah, of course. I mean, he *is* busy, so I'll drive to him so we can spend time together, and we'll go out on a proper date next week." You head over; he might have some food, or a drink, or maybe convince you to bring some, and he'll pay you back? (Insert eye roll here.)

Then the charm commences, the looks, the compliments, the little touches. Well you can figure out what comes next. He tells you "you're different," he "wants a relationship," he's "never done this before." Then there's the promise that he'll see you again and call you later. Oh, and he will; he will call you that day, just less and less for the coming days. And then the busies really sets in. He's been busy, so he hasn't been able to call, text, FaceTime, or make another date. All those things he could do last week but can't this week. Then it just stops. The communication comes to a screeching halt. You, as the woman, start to feel the crazy. What happened? Why? What did I do? Did he lie? Was I duped? The answer is yes.

You played into is plan, gave him what he wanted, and what did you end up with? Confusion. Don't feel bad now. It's happened to the best of us. The men, I like to think, must live with their guilt (hahahahaha). But the part that really confuses me is to think that all these men that put all this effort into a one-night stand. Why for only one night? Don't they want to keep getting laid? I've had honest conversations with admitted playboys, and they all say that they are always onto the next best thing. (Little did they know, they just had the best thing: me! What, what.)

So my advice on this one: men, stop lying, deceiving, and playing games. Give the women the respect to make the decision that affects them. Women, expect more, stand your ground, and *do not be "vagina delivery!"* Don't give these men the "delivery in thirty minutes or less, or it's free guarantee."

Reactions May Vary: For Extreme Butthurt, Please Contact Your Doctor

When I knew this was going from blog to book, I contemplated for a while about whether or not I should tell the "main characters," the men that inspired my writing. I decided it was the right thing to do, and with all the varied reactions I got, it turned out to be the perfect ending.

I first had to decide who I was even going to make the effort to contact. I decided it was for sure the guys that are in the "Leading Men" chapter. I mean, those guys had enough impact on my life; they had whole story written about them. Most of the leading men are also throughout the other chapters as well, so I figured the second requirement was reoccurring roles throughout the stories. The third was anyone that I was still in some kind of relative contact with. So with those in mind, I made a mental note and started the task.

The first phase was the text messages, so I poured a glass of wine and dusted off those old unused contacts and away I went. I sent them all out one night and sat back not knowing where it was going to go.

Texas: "All I ask is that you keep my name out of it." I told him that it wasn't an issue. He would never be referred to as anything but "Texas," and there shouldn't be any surprise since he had read everything I had written about him (until now). He said thank you, and that was it. No love lost with that one, not even the facade of general politeness, all business and to the point.

Mr. Mechanic: Oh lord nothing was ever easy with Mr. M, and he sure wasn't going to let this one go the way of Texas. His initial response was his full name so that his "royalty checks can be made out to and let me know when you need my address to mail my check." I reminded Mr. M that he had never been referred to as anything other than Mr. Mechanic, and therefore, "his name" wasn't entitled to anything.

True to form, he called me a few minutes later. He was at work and apparently decided it was time to chat after months of not talking. I don't know if Mr. M does it to be cruel, to share, to brag, or to process, but he started telling me about a woman he dated that was a New York Times best seller and a relationship counselor. To which my reply was, "It didn't work out, did it?" "Nope, she was completely f——up." I am so happy that he always remains consistent in his behavior and one of his stories, You, Me, and Your Ex Makes Three: He was getting called at work and told me he would call me later.

I told him I'd hold my breath. He found me on one of the dating apps and started writing me on there also. I swear he should medal in "screwing with Samantha." He was typing some nonsense, and I told him that I understand that he doesn't like or approve of my writing and that had a huge impact on why we weren't dating. He replied and said that isn't the only reason. Well yeah, obviously. I told him it was happening whether he liked or not, and that was the last time I heard from him. You see, looking back is the gift of hindsight. I should have cut things off with him in fall of 2017, and here we are smack in 2019 long overdue for a "system purge."

Mr. Hopscotch: His reaction was surprising! He was and is hugely supportive with the whole thing. He told me he was proud and impressed and hoped that it did really well. He told me to tell him my tour dates, and he could make surprise appearances to sign the book! I promise ladies he's quite the looker, so you all wouldn't be disappointed. He did say that he wished that his portion was in a more positive light, but he was excited any way. He has checked in with through the process to see how it was going and even offered creative input for the cover art. Sorry, Mr. Hopscotch, I'm not using a cartoon penis with a face as my book cover. Though I did like his suggestions for a whole "RescueSam" series and podcast.

Mr. One and Done: I see him fairly often at work, so I told him in person the next time I saw him. He wasn't excited when he found out about the blogs to begin with, so I had no idea how he was going to take the book idea. His initial reaction wasn't great; he was borderline mad. He told me, "I still don't even think it's me you wrote about. Those stories aren't about me." Sorry to tell you I very much knew who I wrote about and what happened. After, he calmed down, and he did tell me he thought it was cool it was happening and that the hoped I made a ton of money. Well, that's better than denial and yelling.

The Dude: His reaction was exactly what you would expect from the happy, chill guy. His response when I told him it was being published and he was in it was, "I'm down. Never been in a book. Might get popular LOL. That's cool. Happy for ya. U r doing what ya wanna do." I reminded him I would never release his information, so it would be hard to get popular when no one but him and I know it's about him. He told me I was a strong, beautiful woman and that I should go and be "the strong woman you are meant to be." I was surprised at his kind and inspiring words. So thank you, Dude. I think I will.

One of the last ones was the most surprising because he wasn't even a main character; he is a paragraph. I considered him a friend until... So one night, he saw a Facebook post about my book being accepted by two publishers and that it was actually happening. He left a comment asking, "What book?" I texted him directly and said that I had turned my blogs into a book, and they were going to be published. "Surprise you're going to be in a book." Holly hell, I never envisioned the wrath I was about to get.

He told me that I needed to ask his permission and that I should have given him warning. I kindly reminded him that it wasn't hitting bookstores tomorrow, so this actually was warning. Then I also reminded him that I used no identifying information so that technically, I didn't have to ask his permission. We went back and forth for a bit, and then I stopped responding. He decided he wasn't done with this and texted my best friend, McGruff, and told her that he believed that I was "exploiting men for money," "I had to ask his permission," and many more very unkind things. He demanded to her that I take out anything in reference to him. Now I could have taken out his paragraph, and it wouldn't have really changed the story or the content, but now it was about principle. I said nothing but kind words about him; he was getting notice, and well frankly, he's not the boss of me.

If I am willing to sacrifice relationships, like with Mr. M, to maintain the integrity of my writing, I'll be damned if I am now going to bow to his request because he is feeling some kind of irrational way. He told me, "I guess Sam is just going to do what Sam is going to do." That he was correct about.

I am going to tell my story the way I experienced it, the way it happened to me, my truth, my story, to my readers. I do this for me, to share what I have gone through, good, bad, indifferent, and everything in between. Too many, people are scared to share what they have experienced because someone told them they shouldn't, and far too often, those that are trying to control the narrative are the ones doing the damage in the first place.

The guys that were the angriest about me writing and publishing were the ones that hurt me the most or acted the worst; I can understand why they wouldn't want it. Who wants their worst behavior documented, printed, and presented to the world to read? It's very hard to deny what you've done when it's in black and white. I do hope that they use this as a learning lesson of what not to do and how not to treat a woman.

Not all men are bad, and not all women are innocent. I just write from a hetero-female's perspective because that is what I am and what I live. I have learned a lot from facing my own behavior on the screen. I can see my own mistakes, and I, for sure, have used this to reflect and grow. I am hoping that along with being entertained and relatable, that you can also take my mistakes and hopefully save yourself from some of the blunders and mistakes I've made. Though reflectively each one of those mistakes was a lesson to be learned and a pathway that brought me to this point.

It doesn't seem like dating is going to improve with the coming generations, so we have to adapt and overcome. It will be a continuous process, and I have a feeling this won't be the last time I would ask, "Is this even dating anymore?"

ABOUT THE AUTHOR

Samantha Holland has been in Emergency Medical Services for over sixteen years now and is also a full-time teacher. She lives in California where she works full-time, dates full-time, writes part-time, and is a single parent to two beautiful fur babies, Jack and Jill.

After finding herself thrown back into being single, she decided to experience life for all it has to offer, including loving, losing, and learning the lessons that come with it.

Samantha started blogging two years ago after her second divorce, wanting to share her dating experiences with others. In her blog, *RescueSam The Tragedies and Follies of Dating in Your 30s*, Samantha documented her constant personal evolution and adventures in the world of dating.

After hundreds of dates in this modern, dating-app world, Samantha knew that her struggles were just beginning and had to be shared with the world. With her first book, *"RescueSam: Is This Even Dating Anymore?"* Samantha continues her own odyssey within the world of dating. Those adventures continue to feed her blog and, hopefully, inspire many books to come.

CPSIA information can be obtained
at www.ICGtesting.com
Printed in the USA
LVHW051030040720
659731LV00004B/443